THE MACMILLAN
RELIGIOUS EDUCATION COURSE **BOOK 3**

LIVING
A FAITH

DAVID SELF

M
MACMILLAN
EDUCATION

CONTENTS

Introduction 3

Term One

Birth and Baptism
  1 What is a baby? 4
  2 What's in a name? 6
  3 Child baptism 8
  4 John the Baptist 10
  5 Believers' baptism 12

Coming of Age
  6 Becoming yourself 14
  7 The Hindu sacred thread
     ceremony 16
  8 Bar mitzvah and bat mitzvah 18
  9 Christian confirmation 20
 10 The Sikh amrit ceremony 22

Term Two

Daily Life
 11 Buddhism: the Middle Way 24
 12 The Pillars of Islam 26
 13 The five Ks of Sikhism 28
 14 The Ten Commandments 30
 15 The Beatitudes 32

Faith in Action
 16 Christian prayer 34
 17 Christian worship 36
 18 Monks and nuns 38
 19 Social action 40
 20 Preaching the faith 42

Term Three

Getting Married
 21 Love and marriage 44
 22 Hindu and Sikh marriages 46
 23 Kiddushin: the Jewish wedding
     ceremony 48
 24 Marriage in the Anglican
     Church 50
 25 Till death us do part? 52

Looking Ahead
 26 The problem of suffering 54
 27 No easy answers 56
 28 Cremation 58
 29 Burial 60
 30 Hereafter 62

Conclusions 64

Acknowledgements 64

INTRODUCTION

This is the third book of a three-year course in Religious Education. In this part of the course, we shall be studying the impact of a religious faith on daily life and what the major world faiths have to say about the greater moments of birth, adolescence, marriage and death: the so-called 'rites of passage'. It has not been assumed that the student of this course professes any particular faith or indeed any faith at all.

The course has been arranged in thirty units of study. These units are presented in groups of five and may be studied in order over the course of three terms (as shown opposite). It is not necessary, however, to study them in this order. In order to suit local syllabuses, the different groups of units can be used in other sequénces and units from the other two books of the course may be introduced into this particular year's study. It is hoped that some groups or individuals will wish to explore at least some of the topics in greater depth than is possible in what is intended to be a concise course for use in schools where only limited time is assigned to Religious Education.

It is assumed that each student has access to a Bible. Bible references are given in this form: Exodus 11: 1–7. This indicates the Book of Exodus, chapter eleven, verses 1 to 7.

Rather than use the exclusively Christian terms BC and AD, the terms BCE and CE have been preferred. These stand for 'before the Common Era' and 'Common Era'. The Common Era begins with the year AD 1.

To involve more than one person in a classroom reading of the text, a number of semi-dramatised passages have been included. It may be possible to cast and rehearse these in advance of the lesson. A number of other exercises have been suggested. Several of these might usefully be repeated on topics other than those where they are first suggested. Discussion points might be explored first in small groups (perhaps with notes being made of queries and conclusions), with the small groups later reporting back to the whole class.

However it is used, it is hoped that *The Macmillan Religious Education Course* will lead to an understanding and appreciation of some of the ideas and teachings that have guided, inspired and encouraged different peoples and individuals through the ages.

David Self

1 · WHAT IS A BABY?

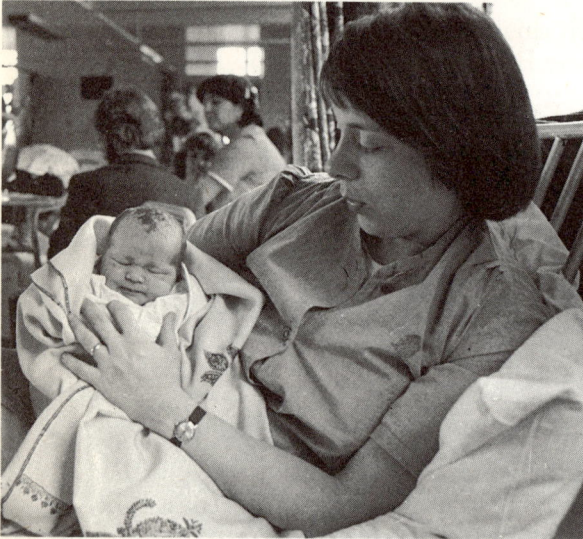

'What happened was my mum sat down and said, "How would you like a baby brother or sister?" I said I wouldn't mind and she said, "Well, you're going to have one."And she said, "Have a feel of my tummy – can you feel it kicking in there?" And I could.'

'Babies are nuisances because they untidy something you have just tidied or wake up in the middle of the night and bawl their heads off. The nice thing about them is that they go to sleep in the afternoon.'

'Babies are horrible bald things. I can't imagine *me* looking like that.'

'Babies, to me, are very soft, podgy little things. When they are about one year old they look exactly the same as one another. You can never tell that when a little helpless baby is born it might be an international soccer player.'

'We were waiting downstairs, drinking some coffee or something and my mum was having the baby upstairs. Then, after they'd cleaned up and everything, we were allowed to go up and look at him. He was a little thing, all wrinkled up. That was the first time I saw him, about only half an hour after he was born.'

To talk about...

1   Can you make a collection of photographs of your class or group when you were all babies? If possible, organise the display without letting each other know the identity of each photograph. How many can you identify? Have you developed as might have been expected?
2   What thoughts, opinions and questions do you have about babies?
Do you like or dislike them?
What are the worst things about them?
What does the word 'vulnerable' mean?
How are babies vulnerable?
Do you find their vulnerability appealing, boring, attractive or frightening?
Have you ever seen or held a really young baby? Can you describe him or her?
'Boys are, on the whole, rather nicer and more protective to babies than girls are.'
(Dr Constance Roberts, child psychiatrist)
Do you agree with that opinion?
3   Can you imagine the feelings of a mother just after her baby has been safely born?
What do fathers think of their babies?
What kinds of things would affect how each parent feels?

Prayer Before Birth

This is a very short part of a poem by Louis Macneice called 'Prayer Before Birth':

I am not yet born; console me.
I fear that the human race may with tall walls wall me,
    with strong drugs dope me, with wise lies lure me,

on black racks rack me, in blood-baths
roll me.

I am not yet born; provide me
With water to dandle me, grass to grow for
me, trees to talk
   to me, sky to sing to me, birds and a
white light
      In the back of my mind to guide me.

Suppose you had been able to make your own 'Prayer Before Birth'. What would you have prayed for protection from? What gifts and strengths might you have prayed to be given? What might you have prayed about your own character? What might you have prayed, in advance, to be forgiven about?

Write your own 'Prayer Before Birth' (or write a future 'Prayer Before Birth' for your own child).

The miracle of birth

A Jewish viewpoint:

> The days of Biblical miracles are long past. The sea does not divide for us, and the blast of the shofar does not shatter the walls of a city. But the greatest miracle occurs a thousand times every day. The miracle of birth.
>
> Birth is a double miracle for Jews. First is the miracle of life itself, the creation of a new human being. Second, although this miracle has occurred billions of times in the past, each birth brings forth a totally new, totally different individual.
>
> The Talmud teaches: 'Man stamps many coins from the same mould, and every coin is exactly the same. But God has stamped many people from the same mould [the mould of Adam], yet not one is like his fellow man. Therefore, one must say, "For my sake was the world created."'

Harry Gersh

(The *Talmud* is a collection of Jewish writings, 'an anthology of wisdom'.)

The birth of a Jewish child is a time of joy for all Jewish people:

> For us, to rejoice means to eat together in happiness. Not alone. We want the whole family there. Mother and father, grandmothers and grandfathers, brothers and sisters – and if it is a big celebration, uncles and aunts and cousins, too. In fact, when we celebrate we celebrate with the Jewish community. They are not merely our people but sort of our family spread very wide. And there are always ceremonies, candles and wine, blessings and prayers. For we are not alone in time. We are linked with God in our lives and in the life of our people. We celebrate His being with us now and His having made the celebration possible for us.

Harry Gersh

And, as we shall see, the birth of a baby is a time for celebration for members of all faiths.

Registering a birth

In England and Wales, the birth of a newborn baby must be registered within 21 days of the birth at the Registrar of Births, Marriages and Deaths 'for either the district where the baby was born or district where the parents (or mother if not married) usually live'. That is the only legal requirement.

Why do you think many people, especially those who believe in a religious faith, want to do more to mark the birth of a baby?

5

2·WHAT'S IN A NAME?

Suppose there is a person (perhaps someone who lives several houses away from you) who knows you only by sight. How must they think of you? Just as 'that kid'?

But 'that kid' could mean anyone. You know you are not just anyone. You are yourself, a unique individual.

One important difference between yourself and other people is your name.

Your personal name identifies you. Your 'surname' identifies your family. One or more of your names may identify your people. For example, if you are called Singh or Kaur, you are very likely to be a Sikh. If one of your names is Muhammad you are likely to be a Muslim. Certain names like O'Reilly and Cohen also suggest to which people you belong.

Names also have their own meanings. In Scotland and Ireland *Mac* and *Mc* mean 'son of' – so Macdonald means 'son of Donald'. In German, *sohn* at the end of a name has the same meaning – so Mendelssohn means 'son of Mendel'.

Ben is a Hebrew word also with that meaning. In Aramaic it becomes *Bar* – so Bar-Abbas means 'son of Abbas'. In Arabic, *Ibn* has that meaning.

British (or Anglo-Saxon) surnames are usually one of four types:
1 those which indicate the name of a parent or other ancestor (e.g Johnson)
2 those which indicate where a family once lived (e.g. Tree, Green, Mill, or a particular place name)
3 the occupation or status of an ancestor (e.g. Cooper, Miller, Lord)
4 those which remember a nickname or description of an ancestor (e.g. Longfellow, Small, Wise)

The meanings of many names can be discovered by consulting the *Penguin Dictionary of Surnames* or *The Oxford Dictionary of English Christian Names*.

To talk about...
What would you like to be called if you could easily change your name?
Which names do you not like? Why?
Which nicknames show popularity and which unpopularity? If you have a nickname, do you like having it?
Is your own name important to you? Do you dislike it when people get it wrong? Try to discover its meaning.
Names sometimes come into or go out of fashion. In 1600 (in England) the commonest personal names were Thomas, Mary, John, Elizabeth, William and Anne. Names such as Gail, Gary and Marilyn are all twentieth century inventions.

Which are the most common names in your school?

Choosing a name
Nowadays many people choose names for a new baby simply because they like the sound of the name. Some names are chosen because they are 'in fashion', while at other times a baby is called after a relative or even a television or pop star.

Jewish children are usually given two

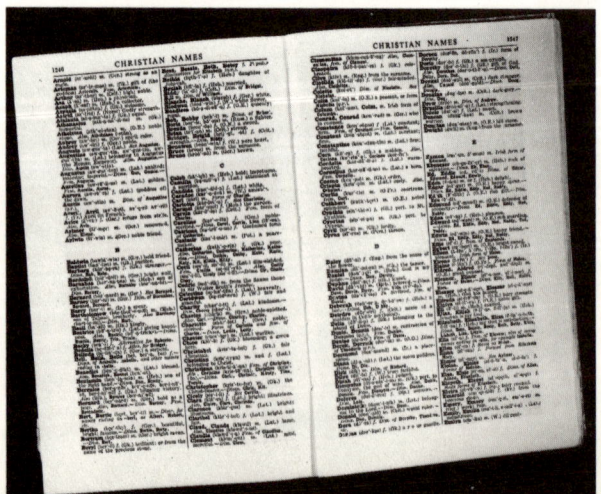

names. One will be a name in the language of the country in which the family lives, the other will be a Jewish or Hebrew name.

Christians often choose names from the Bible for their children.

Muslims say, 'The best method of choosing a name is to consult the holy book, the Qur'an.' So they choose names which appear in that book (many of which also appear in the Jewish and Christian holy books). For example: Yussef (which is Arabic for Joseph) or Ibrahim (Abraham). Names which have special meanings are also chosen. For example, Abdul Rachman means 'the servant of the Most Gracious'. Quite often the name of the holy prophet of Islam, Muhammad, is made part of the boy's name.

Girls may be given one of the names the Prophet gave to his daughters (e.g. Zenob or Fatima).

Giving a name

In many religions, there is a special ceremony when the name is given to the baby. For example, in Reform synagogues, Jewish girls are given their names during the Friday evening service some weeks after their birth.

The Sikh naming ceremony

Just as we have seen that the birth of a baby is a time for celebration in the Jewish faith (unit 1), so it is in the Sikh religion.

'It is a time of joy, of great joy,' according to one Sikh. 'The whole family gets together to give thanks to God for the great gift.'

The relatives and friends visit the family, bringing presents for the baby. In return the father gives a little present (usually something that tastes sweet) to the visitors in return, to show his joy. When the mother and baby first go to the Sikh temple, the gurdwara, the baby will also be given presents, usually including a small copy of the Sikh holy book (the Guru Granth Sahib), a tiny bracelet and something sweet to eat.

Sikhs also have a special way of choosing their baby's name. It can be done anywhere where there is a copy of the Guru Granth Sahib. (Sikhs say that wherever the book is, there is a gurdwara.) Often, however, the ceremony is performed in an actual gurdwara.

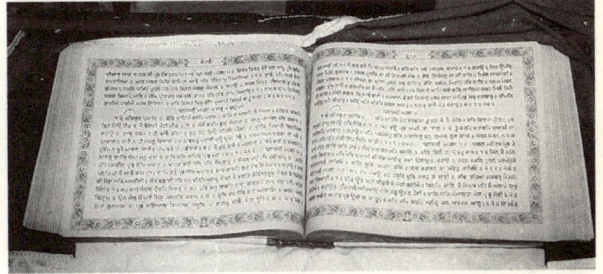

The holy book is opened at any page. The first letter of the first hymn (or other writing) at the top of the left hand page is then chosen as the first letter of the baby's first name. The name does not have to be chosen there and then, but later the family will tell the congregation at the gurdwara the name they have chosen and ask the congregation to accept that name.

Sikhs are also given another name. For boys, this is Singh (which means, literally, lion) and for girls, Kaur (meaning princess). Singh is a reminder to Sikh men that they must be brave, Kaur is a sign of the importance of women. All Sikhs have one or other of these names to show that all Sikhs are equal.

In the West, some Sikhs take a third name to prevent confusion (e.g. in schools where otherwise there might be boys from several families all known as Singh).

Project

Collect newspaper and magazine cuttings that illustrate naming ceremonies and make a montage poster.

For example, you might include accounts of the naming of ships or locomotives; birth announcements from local or national newspapers or from church magazines. If possible, look for ethnic newspapers. What relevant cuttings can you find there?

3·CHILD BAPTISM

For Christians, baptism is both a naming and a 'joining' ceremony. If the person being baptised is a baby, it is when he or she is given their Christian name. It is also the occasion when the person becomes a member of the Christian church. In this way, all Christians are equal. All the branches of the Christian church have some form of baptism service except the Salvation Army and the Society of Friends (Quakers).

Another word for baptism is christening, but the older word and the one used in the New Testament is baptism.

Most Christian churches (e.g. Roman Catholic, Orthodox and many Protestant ones) baptise children while they are still babies. For example, in the Russian Orthodox church, babies are baptised when they are eight days old. However, some Christians believe in *adult baptism* (see unit 5).

Godparents

This is how the Church of England describes what godparents need to do and to be:

> A baby cannot express its own wishes about being baptised, nor can it make the promises to follow Christ that are required at baptism. So each child has the promises made on its behalf by its parents and godparents.
>
> Godparents (sometimes called sponsors) are friends chosen by the parents to share with them in supporting the child in the Christian life until such time as it can make the promises for itself at the service of Confirmation. The Church requires at least three godparents: two of the same sex as the child, and one of the opposite sex. They should be baptised and confirmed members of the Church.

What happens?

Baptism takes place at a *font*. A font need only be a simple basin to hold the water used during the ceremony but often it is a sort of stone basin standing on a short pedestal. It usually stands near the west

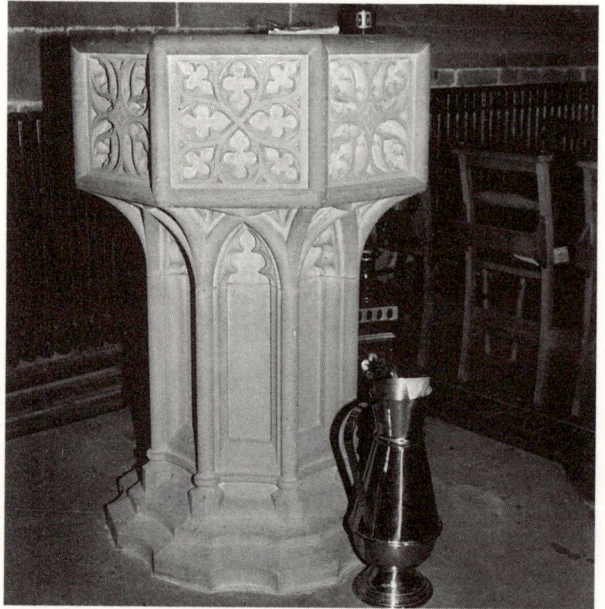

end (or main entrance) of a church. This is because baptism marks the entry of the person into membership of the church.

At one time, baptism was generally a separate service for just the family, godparents and friends of the person being baptised. Now the church is returning to an earlier tradition of holding baptisms during ordinary Sunday services when the baby can be welcomed into the wider family of all the church members.

In the Church of England (when its new Alternative Service Book is used), baptism begins with a reminder of the duties of the parents and godparents:

> The priest says:
> Children who are too young to profess the Christian faith are baptized on the understanding that they are brought up as Christians within the family of the Church...

Parents and godparents, the *children* whom you have brought for baptism *depend* chiefly on you for the help and encouragement *they need*. Are you willing to give it to *them* by your prayers, by your example, and by your teaching?

Parents and godparents:
I am willing.

Following this, the priest again speaks to the godparents:

Therefore I ask these questions which you must answer for yourselves and for *these* children.

Do you turn to Christ?
Answer: I turn to Christ.
Priest: Do you repent of your sins?
Answer: I repent of my sins.
Priest: Do you renounce evil?
Answer: I renounce evil.

The priest then dips his thumb in the water and traces the sign of the cross on the baby's forehead saying, 'Do not be ashamed to confess the faith of Christ crucified.'

Then follows the actual baptism. The priest blesses the water and a little is poured over the baby's head as the priest says the name of the baby:

Name (e.g. Andrew John), I baptise you in the name of the Father, and of the Son and of the Holy Spirit.

And the godparents answer, Amen.

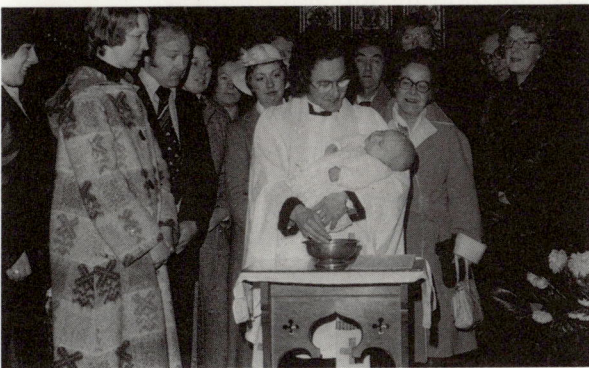

Following this, the newly baptised child is welcomed into not just that local 'family' of the church but into the world-wide church:

Priest: God has received you by baptism into his Church.

All: We welcome you into the Lord's Family.
We are members together of the body of Christ; we are children of the same heavenly Father; we are inheritors together of the kingdom of God.
We welcome you.

Some people question whether it is right to baptise a person before he or she is old enough to want to be baptised – especially as in the early years of the church people were baptised when they were adults (although the New Testament does mention 'whole households' being baptised).

This is what one Church of England priest, Father Gordon James says:

> Babies can't decide *anything* for themselves. That doesn't stop parents deciding what is good for them. The right things to eat, when to go to bed and so on. If they love their baby and if they believe in Jesus, they want to do their best for their child. It's perfectly natural for loving parents to want their child to grow up in the faith.

Projects

1 In pairs, improvise a conversation between the two parents of a young baby. Both believe in Christianity. One wants to have their baby baptised; the other thinks they should wait until he/she is old enough to choose whether he or she wants to be baptised...

2 Improvise a second conversation in which two parents (having decided to have their baby son baptised) are now trying to choose god-parents. One wants rich Aunt Jane (who never goes to church) to be his godmother; the other parent wants his/her younger sister Anne (who is only 16 but goes regularly to church) to be godmother...

3 Write a letter in which a vicar tries (tactfully) to tell two parents that they should choose Christian believers to be godparents of their child and not the people they have suggested.

4·JOHN THE BAPTIST

...Suddenly he'd become one of those people everyone was talking about. A strange, wild-looking man, he was said to wear only a rough garment made from camels' hair and to live on insects and wild honey. He was preaching out in the desert, to the east of the River Jordan. Soon, crowds began making the journey out there to see him and to hear what he'd got to say. And what was he preaching? Nothing that would make him popular...

'Repent! You're a generation of vipers!' he
  began.
'So what do we do about that?' someone
  asked.
'If you own two coats, give one away to the
  poor.'
Two tax collectors spoke up. 'What should
  we do?'
'Don't take a penny more than is your
  right.' The crowd approved.
'And what about us?' asked a small group
  of soldiers.
'Do no violence to anyone.' The soldiers
  looked confused. One tried to laugh. 'And
  don't moan about your pay,' added the
  preacher.
Later, many people (including some who
  had gone only out of curiosity) agreed to
  be led by John down into the muddy river
  and, for a moment or two, to be held
  under the water by him.

To find out how the Bible records these events, read Mark 1:4–8 and also Luke 3:7–14. What other information does Matthew give us? (Matthew 3:4–12).

Locusts are in fact a useful source of food in areas where meat is scarce, as they contain both fat and protein. After being mixed with honey to take away the bitterness, they need to be cooked before being eaten.

At that time, baptism was the way non-Jews could become a member of the Jewish religion. It showed that the person was making a new start or change of direction; and it was a sign of repentence, a symbol of the washing away of sin.

So why did crowds of people who were already Jews, including members of the most respected classes, want to go through all this?

Why did John seem important?
1 John was himself a member of the 'upper' or priestly class. His father, Zacharias, had been a priest.
2 According to tradition, this was where the great Jewish prophet, Elijah, had preached eight hundred years before.
3 Elijah had also dressed in rough clothes made from camel hair. (For more information about Elijah, see Book 2, unit 9.)
4 Many Jews believed that Elijah would return to earth to announce the coming of a saviour or Messiah who would save his people. (For more information about the idea of the Messiah, see Book 1, unit 9.)
5 John said he was a messenger, preparing the way for someone more important.

So what did all this suggest about John? Did it seem right to pay attention to him? And what would getting baptised mean to a Jew, if all this was so?

Write...

Suppose you are a member of the upper class, living in Jerusalem. Out of curiosity, you and a friend decide to go to see what John has got to say for himself. You try to listen without drawing attention to yourselves. Gradually what he says begins to make sense. Your friend disagrees...

Write a description of your visit to the Baptist and the conversation you have with your friend. (Does either of you go forward to be baptised?)

THE BAPTISM OF JESUS

Jesus and John were cousins. John was six months older than Jesus. (For an account of the birth of John, read Luke, chapter one.) But note that it was their mothers who were related. In Jewish society at that time, it was natural that a family should live close to the father's family – so Jesus grew up with Joseph's family in Nazareth while John lived in the Judean hills, ninety miles to the south. There is no record of Jesus and John having met before the former's baptism. However, some people think it is unlikely they would not know each other.

Read the account of how Jesus was baptised (Mark 1:9–12) and, using that evidence, answer as many of these questions as you can:
1 Where did Jesus come from?
2 Do you think John and Jesus knew each other?
3 What was seen after Jesus came out of the water?
5 What was heard after Jesus came out of the water?
5 Who saw the sign?
6 Who heard the voice?
Now read Matthew's account. (Matthew

3:13–17.) Do we get the same answers? What else does Matthew tell us?

From either of these accounts, can we tell if Jesus knew he was the Messiah *before* being baptised?

Finally read John's account. (John 1:29–34.)

What answers do we now get to the six questions? Did John know who was to be the Messiah?

CHRISTIAN BAPTISM

Jesus did not baptise people himself – but note what were his last words to his apostles (or disciples), according to Matthew (Matthew 28:18–20).

The New Testament tells us what happened at Pentecost when the apostles first spoke in Jerusalem. Peter said, 'Each one of you must turn away from your sins and be baptised in the name of Jesus...and you will receive God's gift, the Holy Spirit.' (See also Book 1, unit 23.)

The New Testament also tells us that baptism means
1 'death to the old way of life'
2 'the gift of the Spirit' (Christians believe that through the Holy Spirit, God is with those who believe in Him and gives them strength), and
3 the entry into membership of the Christian church

Sacraments

From then on, baptism (whether as baby or adult) became the normal way of joining the church and is known as a 'sacrament'. The word means both a sign and a promise or pledge. A Christian teacher, St Augustine, described a sacrament as 'an outward and visible sign of an inward and spiritual grace'. Water is the outward sign; the inward meaning being 'the gift of the Spirit'.

The other great sacrament is Holy Communion. (What is the outward sign then?)

5 · BELIEVERS' BAPTISM

The story of the baptism of Jesus by John forms the basis for the Christian baptism ceremony we studied in unit 3. However, not all Christian churches baptise young babies and some believe that, instead of sprinkling a little water on the person's forehead, the person should be immersed completely in water. (The word 'baptism' comes from a Greek one which can mean either 'to dip' or 'to immerse'.)

The Baptist churches

Members of the Baptist churches are among those Christians who believe in adult baptism. They say it is right to baptise only people who have decided for themselves that they believe in Jesus and that they want to be baptised. Baptists therefore speak of 'believers' baptism'. Obviously, they say, a small baby cannot decide what he or she believes about Jesus.

They also believe that baptism should be like that undergone by Jesus – so they have baptism by total immersion and not by 'sprinkling'.

NB Baptists do have a ceremony to mark the birth of a child called a 'service of dedication'. It is partly a thanksgiving for the birth of the child when not only the parents and family give thanks but all the church members join in. The service also marks the dedication of the parents to the child when they make a vow (or promise) to bring their child up 'in the discipline and the instruction of the Lord'. Again all the church members promise to join in caring for that child.

Believers' baptism

Believers' baptism can take place once a person is thought to be mature enough to make his or her own decision. It can be any time from the age of thirteen upwards. As one Baptist minister, the Reverend Michael Quicke, puts it: 'The person must have come in their own heart and mind to want to make a new start in life. They must want to "turn around" from their past life and must want Jesus to be Lord of their life, to be number one in their life. Having made that decision, they must want to declare it in the way Jesus chose – which means baptism by immersion, in public.'

What happens?

Michael Quicke describes what happens when he conducts 'believers' baptism' in his church in Cambridge:

66 As you look to the front of the church, you'll see there is a pulpit in the middle. That shows the importance we place on reading and preaching the *word* of God, the Bible. In front of it is a pool. It's quite deep – the water comes up to your waist. The pool is often T-shaped, and it's tiled like a swimming pool. There are steps on either side.

At a baptism service, after explaining to everybody how we're obeying Jesus and how he asked us to make new disciples and to baptise them in this way, I go down into the pool. Very often ministers wear normal clothes for this, perhaps white shirt and trousers (white being the colour of new life and pure living); but I wear a special robe so I can get changed quickly afterwards. Men and boy candidates also often wear an ordinary white shirt and trousers but women and girl candidates wear a simple white robe.

I then ask the candidates to come and stand at the top of the steps and the congregation stands to watch. Then I ask each candidate two questions while they stand in public view. I ask whether they repent of their sins and believe in the Lord Jesus Christ; and secondly, whether they promise to follow him and serve God for the rest of their lives.

When they've said 'I do', they come down into the water. They just stand there, their hands folded in front of them. I say, 'On the profession of your repentence towards God and of faith in Our Lord Jesus Christ, I baptise you in the name of the Father and of the Son and of the Holy Spirit. Amen.'

And I very gently lean them backwards into the water so they go under the water for a moment and then, as they come up out of the water, they go up the steps on the other side and a special friend (called a sponsor) is there to greet them and, as they stand there, we sing a verse of a hymn and the next person comes to be baptised. 99

For Baptists, the water used in baptism is not just a symbol of cleansing and of new life but, by being immersed in it, the person being baptised is linked with Jesus. 'It is a kind of burial, a burial beneath the water, identifying yourself with the death of Jesus, and the coming to new life.' As their service says, 'As the body is buried under water and rises again, so shall the bodies of the faithful be raised by the power of Christ.'

Projects

1 Make a sequence of drawings to illustrate what happens at believers' baptism, and write short (but precise) captions for each 'frame'.

2 'Adult or infant baptism?' Discuss what is to be said for and against each.

3 Discuss whether you think total immersion is necessary for Christian baptism.

(Note: although Christians do not all agree on the time and place of baptism, almost all stress how important they believe it to be.)

6·BECOMING YOURSELF

Growing up

As we grow up, we want freedom. Freedom to do things on our own, without older people (especially parents) telling us what we should do and when we should do it.

Fred has just come downstairs, on his way out...

Mother: You came down those stairs like a herd of elephants.

Fred: Trumpety trumpety trump.

Mother: You what?

Fred: Trumpety trumpety...Elephants. The noise elephants make. Oh never mind.

Mother: I don't know what you're talking about. Oh and look. I don't know what you want to go out looking like that for. I put your school blazer out. Specially. Your blazer'd be nice for going to the theatre.

Fred: It's not a theatre, Mum. It's a concert. A pop concert. A *jazz* concert. Can't go in school uniform. No one would.

Mother: And look. You're to be back by ten o'clock. Ten o'clock mind.

Fred: But Mum...

Mother: No buts. Ten o'clock.

Fred: But it may not have finished then. An' even if it has, there'll be people to talk to, we'll go for a coffee.

Mother: Fred, you're not going out with girls are you? Fred. Now look, Fred. You're not messing about with girls are you? Fred?

Fred (*angry*): Mum...

Mother: Fred, I'm your mother, Fred.

Fred (*angrier*): Mum!

Mother: Fred! Fred! (*the front door slams*) Fred!

That may seem an extreme case. These are actual comments from young teenagers:

> My Mum always wants me in at half past ten – and every time I go out to a Youth Club or something like that, we always have an argument about what time I'm going to be in – half past ten – and I'll say it ends at eleven and she says, 'Well, you're too young, you should be in bed at nine o'clock or half past nine.' Every time we have an argument about that.

> My Mum always makes me go to bed about half past nine. She says, 'It's school tomorrow – you've got to get up' and even if there's a film or anything on she won't let me stay up. I've always got to go to bed at half past nine unless it's in the holidays.

"Good heavens no, dear—of course we weren't worried."

To talk about...

What situations and experiences are you reminded of by these comments?

Improvise a scene between a parent and teenage child involving a disagreement from your own experience.

Improvise a conversation between two or three fathers or mothers about their teenage children.

Remind yourself of how a Jewish family observes the Sabbath. (See Book 2, unit 16.) Now discuss this situation:
A Jewish boy has been invited out by his non-Jewish friends on a Friday evening (when, of course, the Sabbath evening meal is eaten). He does not wish to appear 'wet' to his friends. What should he do and say?

Write...
As we grow older, we may 'grow away' from our parents and resent it when they try to order our lives for us. Write about an occasion when you felt your mother or father was interfering in your life or making a rule that was unnecessary. Or when you felt they were treating you as though you were younger than you are.

DUTIES AND RESPONSIBILITIES

As we grow up, we gain more freedom. We need our parents less. At some stage, we may leave home. But we are each still part of a family. That means we have duties and responsibilities to our parents (as well as rights). One day, they may need us.
This is what some religions teach about this matter:

Hinduism
The Bhagavad-Gita (a Hindu holy book) stresses a child's duty to parents and the love parents must show to children, but states that it is wrong for one person to try to fulfil someone else's dharma (duties) – it is better to do your own dharma badly than to do another's well.

Judaism
'Honour your father and your mother, so that you may live long in the land the Lord your God is giving you.'
'A person must honour his father in life and in death.'

Islam
'Be kind to parents and near kinsmen and to orphans and to the needy.'

Buddhism
'Father and mother must be hearkened to.'

'A mother will cherish her son because she expects that he will support her and a son loves his mother because she bore him in her womb.'

Do you agree with these teachings? Why – or why not?

Coming of age
We talk of 'coming of age' at 18. (It used to be 21.) But people 'come of age' at different ages for different activities.
When can you legally: see a PG film on your own? buy cigarettes? babysit? drive a car? buy things on hire purchase? get married (with your parents' consent)? vote? buy drinks with a meal in a restaurant?
From these ages, you are an 'adult' so far as that activity is concerned.
In the different religions of the world, there are various ceremonies to mark your 'coming of age' so far as your religion is concerned.
We shall study four of these in the following units.

Civil confirmation ceremonies
These are held in Scandinavia. A special annual 'coming-of-age' ceremony is held for young people who have reached voting age. All are invited to the Town Hall where the civic dignitaries preside, the band plays, refreshments are served....And the whole is preceded by a course in civic responsibilities.
Do you think it would be a good idea for all young people to have a civic 'coming-of-age' ceremony such as this – irrespective of what religious or political beliefs they hold?

7·THE HINDU SACRED THREAD CEREMONY

This Hindu ceremony (called *upanayana*) is performed on boys usually some time between their seventh and twelfth birthdays. Only boys from the top three castes undergo the ceremony.

It is thought of as being a kind of 'second birth' for the boy, an entry into adulthood or maturity and is the most important ceremony in a young Hindu's life.

Before it takes place, the boy has to learn all the duties and responsibilities of an adult Hindu from his *guru* or teacher.

The ceremony

During the actual ceremony, the boy and a Brahmin priest sit on opposite sides of a sacred fire. Prayers and hymns are chanted and the boy has to repeat various prayers after the priest. Then the thread is put on him. It may be either red, white or yellow and is in the form of a loop, made of several strands. It is worn over the left shoulder and across the body to the right hip.

When a boy has received his sacred thread, he begins a period of study under the direction of his guru.

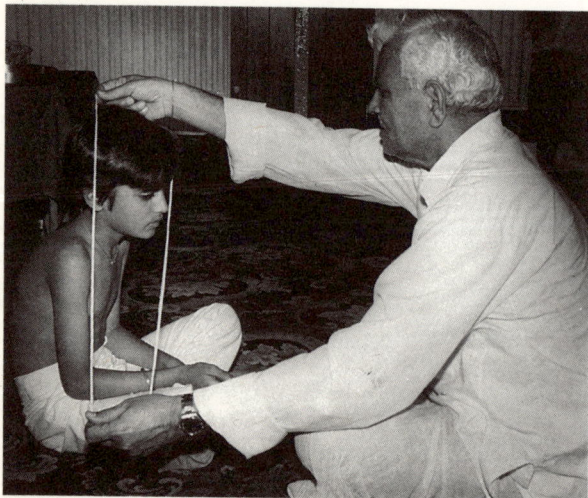

Caste

Every Hindu is born into a class or 'caste'. (The Hindu word is *jati*.)

The four castes are:

1 The priestly caste (the Brahmins)
2 The warrior and ruler caste (the Kshatriyas)
3 The farmer and merchant caste (the Vaishyas)
4 The unskilled worker caste (the Shudras)

Below the caste system are the so-called Untouchables (or Outcasts) who do the lowest jobs.

Traditionally, a Hindu cannot change his or her caste and must marry into the same caste. There are also laws saying which castes can prepare certain foods. Hindus believe it is possible to be born into a higher (or lower) caste in a new life.

Many Indians wish to reform the caste system and the great holy leader Mahatma Gandhi did much to break down its rules.

Daily duties

Once a Hindu boy has received the sacred thread, he is considered an adult and has five daily duties or obligations. These are:

1 To worship God (Om), either directly or through the various gods. A common form of worship is *puja*. This is performed in that part of the home which is set aside as a shrine. (See Book 2, unit 20.) Prayers are said and offerings of food and flowers are made to the god.
2 To respect holy men and holy writings.
3 To honour parents, elders and ancestors.
4 To give shelter and gifts of food and money to the poor.
5 To care for animals and all living things.

For Hindus, religion enters every part of life. For example, this is what a Hindu may

These preparations are important because of the way the Hindus think about the human body. For instance, the head is the highest part of the body, and has to be kept pure; the mouth has to be particularly pure when sacred words are to be spoken. The feet, being the lowest part, do not have to be so pure. Touching a person's feet, especially touching them with your head, is a way of showing respect for him, because it shows that your place is below him. What covers the head has special meaning for Hindus; so displacing or hitting a Hindu's headgear is a great insult. It is even worse if you hit his head with your shoe.
"

To talk about...

1 What are your opinions about the caste system? What can be said in its favour? For example: solidarity between workers in one trade; a 'reward' in the next life or re-incarnation, etc. NB The caste system is not so strong these days, but it continues in many village communities and many Hindus would not think of marrying outside their caste.

2 Plan and improvise an interview in which a Hindu boy or girl explains the sacred thread ceremony to a non-Hindu. Continue the interview to explain what is important to a Hindu about cleanliness, prayer, diet and attitudes to others.

NB Although girls do not undergo this ceremony, Hinduism does honour and respect women in other ways. As *A Handbook of Hinduism* states:

> Hindu statements about the status of women give them an exalted place. The Vedas call a wife the 'bliss-giver' of the family.... Hindu women run the home and control it completely. The average Hindu man has little say in the home and does not help very much in the house, even when his wife is at work. Hindus admire and respect a woman who looks after the family well, does the shopping thriftily, cooks meals on time and still has time to join in the fun they have together.

do at the start of a day (as described in *A Handbook of Hinduism*):

" When he gets out of bed, the right foot touches the ground first, to make a good start to the day. A special prayer may be said as the foot touches the earth, which was created by God.

He cleans his teeth and tongue. In an Indian village, he uses a twig of a special tree, and then throws it away. In towns, disposable toothbrushes do not grow on trees, but Hindus are still very particular about keeping clean.

He takes a bath, in a river, a pool or a bathroom. To a Hindu, having a daily bath has always been an important custom; the ancient cities of the Harappan civilization, built before 2,000 BCE, had elaborate bathrooms and drainage. A Hindu should not have breakfast without saying his prayers, and he should not say his prayers until he has first bathed so that he can meet God in a state of cleanliness. Running water is best for bathing; if he has to use a bathroom, a shower is best because the water runs from the head, which is the highest and purest part of the body, down to the feet.

17

8·BAR MITZVAH AND BAT MITZVAH

Jewish boys 'come of age' on their thirteenth birthday. Jewish girls come of age on their twelfth birthday. (Judaism recognises the fact that girls mature more quickly than boys.)

On his thirteenth birthday, a Jewish boy becomes 'bar mitzvah'; that is, he becomes a 'son of the law' or 'son of the covenant'.

Similarly, on her twelfth birthday, a girl becomes 'bat mitzvah' or 'daughter of the law' or covenant.

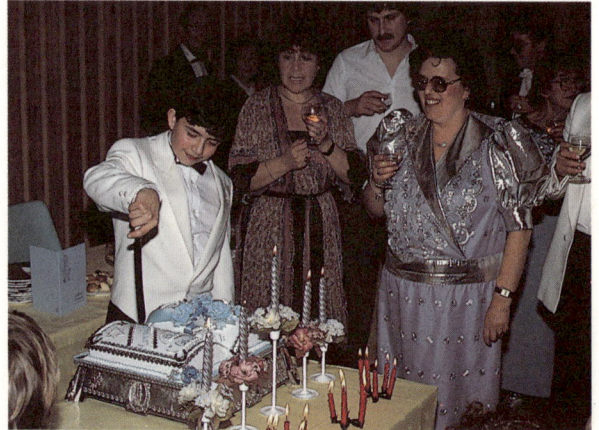

A bar-mitzvah boy cuts his cake at a party after the religious ceremony

Becoming 'bar-mitzvah' at the Western Wall, Jerusalem

Technically, it is wrong to talk about 'bar mitzvah' as if it is a ceremony. It is the person.

From the day on which a boy becomes 'bar mitzvah', he is himself responsible for his own behaviour. Up till then he has been learning the law, learning what is right and what is wrong, and so on. Up till this day, his father has had the duty to encourage him to obey the Torah. (See Book 1, unit 15 and Book 2, unit 4.) Now the boy's behaviour is his own responsibility. He is an adult.

With adulthood come privileges. He may be 'called up' to read part of the Torah in the synagogue or to lead the prayers. By his thirteenth birthday, a Jewish boy should be able to read Hebrew and to chant or read a part of the Torah.

What happens?

Strictly speaking, nothing need happen for a boy to become 'bar mitzvah', just as nothing need happen on your eighteenth birthday for you to become legally of age. However, just as people have found ways of celebrating their eighteenth (and twenty-first) birthdays, so a number of customs have grown up over the last few hundred years to celebrate becoming 'bar mitzvah'.

The most important event happens in the synagogue on the sabbath following the bar mitzvah boy's birthday. Many of his relatives and friends attend the synagogue. During the service, the boy reads or chants a portion of the Torah, wearing his prayer shawl (or *tallith*).

His father will recite a blessing on his son. In this blessing, the father says he will continue to care for his son, but is allowing him to be free to make grown-up decisions – and to accept the consequences.

The rabbi usually gives a special sermon, directed especially to the boy.

Later there is a festive meal or party, given by the parents in their son's honour.

At some time, either in the synagogue, in an afternoon study group or at the party, the boy makes a *derasha*. This is a speech or mini-sermon (or even prayer). It is a 'thank you' to his parents and teachers, and a welcome to the guests.

In Orthodox Jewish communities, where adult males wear *t'filin* at prayer time, the boy will now also do the same.

T'filin are small black leather boxes. They contain certain Biblical passages. The little boxes are tied to the arm and forehead, near the mind. They are worn as a reminder of a commandment in the book Deuteronomy: 'Bind the words of God between your eyes and upon your arm.'

Bat mitzvah

In Progressive or Liberal synagogues, the occasion of a bat mitzvah is just like that of a bar mitzvah.

In Orthodox synagogues, it may take place on a Sunday. Several girls may share a bat mitzvah ceremony.

Becoming bar mitzvah or bat mitzvah is not something that just lasts one day. It is entering a state that lasts for the rest of life.

To talk about...

1 What do you think makes a person a 'grown up'?

2 Apart from taking part in religious ceremonies, what do young people do to try to prove they are grown up?

3 If you had to devise a test or examination that people had to undergo to prove that they were responsible adults, what tasks or questions would it contain? Devise and write an 'entry into adulthood' examination paper.

4 Make a list of all the names of Jewish festivals that you can remember and other words connected with Judaism. In small teams, test each other on their meaning (perhaps using the format of the 'Twenty Questions' game).

9·CHRISTIAN CONFIRMATION

Full membership

Which sorts of organisation have membership cards?

How many different ones can you find?

Which organisations ask you to make a promise when you become a member? For example, the Scouts and Guides? Some supporters' clubs? Social clubs?

Devise a membership card for a school club or society.

'Christ died for all, that those who live might live no longer for themselves but for him who for their sake died and was raised.'

II Corinthians 5:15 (RSV)

Member ....

Minister ....

Membership of the Christian church

We have already seen (units 3 and 5) how people can become members of the Christian church through baptism. For those who believe in adult baptism, baptism brings full membership of the church.

For those who believe in infant baptism, there is another service when church members 'come of age'. This is called *confirmation*. At confirmation, those being confirmed make for themselves the promises that were made on their behalf at baptism. They take on the full responsibility of being adult Christians.

Following this 'renewal of baptismal vows' comes the most important part of the service. The bishop puts his hands on each person's head and says a blessing: 'Confirm, O Lord, your servant...' ('To confirm' means 'to make strong'.) In this way, it is believed the strength and help of the Holy Spirit is given to the person.

In the Church of England, the service begins with hymns, prayers and there is usually a sermon. Then come the two main parts of the service. The first is a renewal of baptismal vows when those who are to be confirmed make for themselves the promises made on their behalf at baptism. This is followed by the act of confirmation:

The Confirmation

The Bishop stands before those to be confirmed and says:

      Our help is in the name of the Lord
All: who has made heaven and earth.
Bishop: Blessed be the name of the Lord
All: now and forever. Amen.

The Bishop stretches out his hands towards them and says:

      Almighty and everliving God, you have given your servants new birth in baptism by water and the Spirt, and have forgiven them all their sins. Let your Holy Spirit rest upon them: the Spirit of wisdom and understanding; the Spirit of counsel and inward strength; the Spirit of

knowledge and true godliness; and let their delight be in the fear of the Lord.
Amen.

The Bishop lays his hand on the head of each candidate, saying:
Confirm, O Lord, your servant *N* with your Holy Spirit.
and each one answers:
Amen.

There is no rule in the Anglican Church as to what age a person should be confirmed. It is usually between the ages of 11 and 16 but of course an older person who wants to join the church can be confirmed at any age (after first being baptised, if he or she has not already been baptised). Once a person has been confirmed, they can receive Holy Communion.

In the Roman Catholic Church, confirmation now usually happens between the ages of 10 and 14, but a Roman Catholic may make his or her first communion before being confirmed (often at about the age of seven or eight, the age at which for many centuries Catholics were confirmed).

In the Orthodox Church, confirmation happens straight after baptism.

Some Protestant churches (e.g. the Methodist, Pentecostal and Baptist Churches) do not have confirmation, but some have services or meetings at which new members are received into the church.

Why confirmation?

Confirmation is based on 'the laying on of hands' mentioned in the New Testament.

For example, we can see from Acts 8:14–17 that new members of the Church were baptised and that then one of the apostles 'laid their hands upon them'. (See also Acts 19:5–6.) Not all Christians believe these references describe 'confirmation services'.

Many Christians believe that they should be confirmed however because:
1 they believe it is mentioned in the Bible
2 the Church has confirmed its members since at least the fourth century CE

3 it is a help, a 'strengthening', and
4 it is a way of showing that you want to enter full membership of the Church.

Note that in the Anglican and Catholic Churches, confirmation is always administered by a bishop. A bishop is made (or 'consecrated') a bishop by at least three other bishops. Those bishops were made bishops by other bishops and many Christians believe this line of succession goes back to the original eleven apostles.

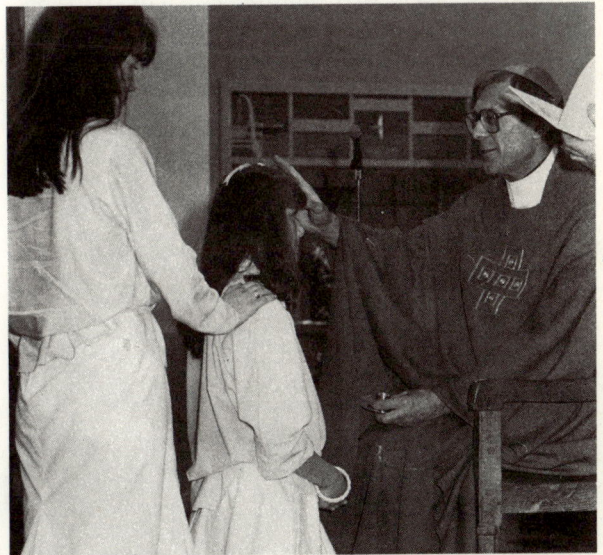

To talk about...

1 Is there anyone in your group who has been confirmed recently? Can they describe what happened? What sort of preparation (or 'training') was there? What happened on the day?
2 How might Christians find it helpful to be confirmed?
3 Why do you think some Christian churches do not think it is necessary?
4 What do you think is the right age for a person to be confirmed?

Drama

Read Acts 8:4–25 carefully. Improvise or script a short play about the visits to Samaria of Philip, Peter and John. (Alternatively you could re-tell the events as a short story in your own words.)

10·THE SIKH AMRIT CEREMONY

In Sikhism, 'coming of age' or entry into full membership of the faith is marked by the amrit ceremony. It is sometimes referred to as baptism. At this ceremony Sikhs are made full members of the Khalsa, the 'brotherhood' of all Sikh believers who vow to keep true to their faith and to serve the community. Men and women are admitted on equal terms.

For the story of the founding of the Khalsa, see Book 2, unit 23.

This is what a Sikh handbook, *The Turban and the Sword of the Sikhs*, says about who may be admitted:

> Any man (or woman) above the age of sixteen, belonging to any race, nationality, speaking any language, is eligible for receiving the baptism but he should be fully conversant with the discipline of a baptized Sikh.

The ceremony takes place in the gurdwara, the Sikh temple (see Book 2, unit 19). Because there are no 'clergymen' or priests in Sikhism, the service is conducted by five adult Sikhs who are already members of the Khalsa. They can be men or women and should be respected members of the congregation. For the ceremony they wear special yellow robes with blue or red sashes. They represent the first members of the Khalsa, known as the *Panj Pyares* ('the beloved five').

> On the day a novice is to be baptized he should take a bath (wash his body and hair), wear absolutely clean clothes and have with him what are called the five Ks (1) *Kesh*: uncut hair (2) *Kanga*: comb (3) *Kirpan*: sword of about 6 inches (4) *Kara*: bracelet (5) *Kaccha*: drawers of special type. The hair

should be tied as a tress-knot on the head and the turban tied on it gracefully. (See unit 13.)

Before the ceremony starts every recipient has to present himself before the *Panj Pyares* in the presence of the Holy Book and take a vow that he will dedicate his mind, body and soul to the Ten Gurus and the *Panth* (the Sikh community). If he does not qualify himself for baptism for some reason or the other, he is told about it, and is advised to come again when he is fully prepared.

The ceremony

This is a description of what happens, taken from the Sikh booklet mentioned above:

> On the altar of the Sikh Temple one always sees the *Adi Guru Granth*: the Holy Book of the Sikhs. In front of the Holy Book all things required for the ceremony of baptism are placed: steel bowl, water, sugar pellets, two-edged sword (see unit 13); and the sacramental food (*karah prashad*) is kept on one side to be distributed after the ceremony is over. Around the steel bowl stand the *Panj Pyares*, and behind them in a semi-circle stand all the novices. Men and women, boys and girls stand in one row.

Prayers are said and a hymn is sung. Then the five Sikhs leading the service start the ceremony.

> They pour the water into the bowl, and then they put some sugar pellets into the water uttering the Name of God while doing so. All the five sit round the bowl in *Vir-asana* (sitting in the pose of an archer ready to let loose an arrow), everyone placing both his hands on the edge of the bowl, clasping it lightly but firmly. From right to left the five ministers then recite in deep meditative tone from memory,

five prayers, one each by turn. Each minister (while reciting the prayer) holds the two-edged sword in his right hand with which he churns the water while he keeps his left hand on the bowl. After he has completed the prayer he hands over the two-edged sword to the next minister. When all the recitations are over the five ministers stand up (holding the steel bowl of baptismal water in their hands) and once more say a prayer of thanksgiving and seek the grace and blessings of God for those who are about to receive the baptism. **"**

NB *Vir-asana* ('the posture of a warrior') shows that they are always ready to defend their faith. The holy water is called *amrit*. Water is the symbol of purity; the sugar or sweetness a symbol of holiness.

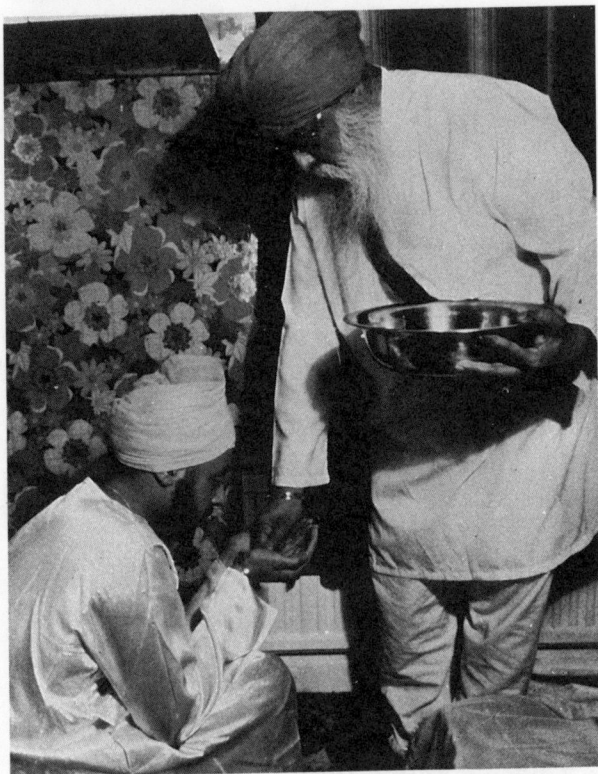

Each person seeking entry to the Khalsa then comes forward in turn to accept 'baptism'. He or she takes the same vir-asana position and then each of the five *Panj Pyares* pours a little amrit into his hands and asks him to drink.

Then amrit is sprinkled on the young person's eyes. This indicates that from then on the baptised Sikh should see no evil. Each of the ministers next places a little amrit on his head. In this way, the most important part of the body is anointed with the holy water.

When all the candidates have been initiated into the Khalsa, a hymn is sung and prayers are said. Then the service ends with everyone sharing the *karah prashad*, the very sweet, holy food of the Sikhs.

It is at this service that Sikhs take the name 'Singh' or 'Kaur' (see unit 2).

To talk about...

1 In what ways is the Sikh amrit ceremony like Christian baptism? How is it different? Some people have suggested that the amrit ceremony is more like Christian confirmation (or adult baptism)? Do you agree?

2 Why is the amrit ceremony important for Sikhs?

3 In which religious ceremonies does water play an important part? Why?

4 Do you think people should *not* be allowed to join a religious faith before a certain age? Or do you think that people will not grow up to be interested in religion if they are not members of a faith?

5 What do you think should happen to people who fail to live up to the rules of their faith? Should there be a punishment?

6 Is it a good or bad idea if we can say to which religion people belong by their appearance?

Conclusions

In the last ten units we have considered some of the ceremonies and customs that accompany birth and coming of age in various faiths. Can you devise a table or wall chart that summarises the main points about Jewish, Christian and Sikh ceremonies? In groups, you could discuss the best ways of arranging the information. How will you show the similarities? And the differences?

11 · BUDDHISM: THE MIDDLE WAY
DAILY LIFE

What is happiness?
Happiness is day-dreaming in class...
Happiness is unlimited supplies of salt-and-vinegar crisps...
Happiness is a hot bath...
Happiness is not having to do what other people say...
Happiness is being with people you like and who like you...
Make your own list to say what you think happiness is.

To talk about...
1 Do you need money to be happy?
2 Does work bring happiness?
3 Does happiness last for only a short time?
4 Who is the happiest person you know? What makes him or her so happy?
5 Can you make other people happy? Who? How?
6 Can you make yourself happy? Can you *find* happiness?

'Enlightenment'
In Book 1, unit 12, we studied how a Hindu prince, Siddartha Gautama, left his palace and wealth, and became a wandering hermit. His aim was to discover why there was so much suffering and unhappiness in the world. Eventually, he sat down under a bhodi tree. One morning, the answer or 'truth' was revealed to him and from then he became known as 'the Buddha' (a word which means 'the enlightened one').

THE MIDDLE WAY

The Buddha's first teaching was that we should follow 'the Middle Way'. By this, he meant that we should avoid all extremes. We should avoid excessive indulgence in the 'pleasures of life' and we should also avoid extreme self-denial.

Much of his other teaching is preserved in numbered lists: the Four Noble Truths, the Eightfold Path and the Five (or Ten) Precepts.

The Four Noble Truths
In particular, the Buddha taught that, in order to understand why there is suffering and unhappiness we should face up to what are called 'The Four Noble Truths':
1 In this world, nothing lasts. Even the happiest moments pass away. Nobody experiences total and permanent happiness or satisfaction. The Buddhist word for the 'unsatisfactoriness' of life is *dukkha* (a word which means 'restlessness' and 'suffering').
2 *Dukkha* happens because people want to keep things; they want more and more and are never satisfied. They become greedy and selfish. If countries become greedy, then this leads to war.
3 *Dukkha* can cease if you overcome your selfishness, greed and hatred.
4 The way to do this is to follow the Eightfold Path. (See below.)

The Eightfold Path
You will see from above that the way to avoiding 'ill' or *dukkha* is to follow the Eightfold Path. This is another way of expressing its steps:

● *Understanding:* People should see clearly what they are doing with life.
● *Thinking:* They should learn to free themselves from the grip of day-dreams so that thoughts can be more clear.
● *Speech:* Talking can be used to say good things and to understand others.

- *Action:* Good acts arise when there is no clinging to the results of actions.
- *Work:* People should try not to take jobs which will harm other living creatures.
- *Effort:* They should try to use their will to cut through difficulties.
- *Mindfulness:* People should pay full attention to what they are doing.
- *Concentration:* They should try to concentrate on becoming one with the situation, whatever it is.

Anne Bancroft

Dharma-chakra

The Dharma-chakra (or Wheel of Law) has eight spokes and is one way of illustrating the Eightfold Path.

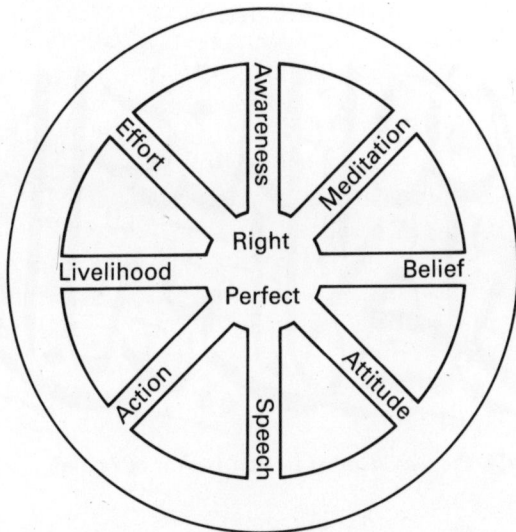

Can you plan and draw a personal 'wheel of law' or 'wheel of life' that shows how you would like to live your life in the coming years?

The Precepts

There are no 'rules' in Buddhism for daily life (like the Ten Commandments).

Buddhists have to make their own decisions about what is their 'Middle Way'. They must learn to understand that whatever they choose to do in any particular situation has its own results – both for the person making the choice and possibly for other people as well.

To help them do 'the best thing' in any situation, Buddhists often make five promises (known as the Five Precepts):

1 Not to kill or harm any living thing.
2 Not to take anything that is not given to you.
3 Not to indulge yourself physically.
4 Not to lie or say anything cruel.
5 Not to drink alcohol or take drugs.

Buddhist monks (and anyone living as a monk for a period of time) make a further five Promises or Precepts (see also unit 18):

6 Not to eat excessively or after midday.
7 Not to be involved in, or to watch dancing, acting or singing.
8 Not to use perfumes or ornaments.
9 Not to use a comfortable bed.
10 Not to accept (or even handle) gold or silver.

To talk about...

Buddhism began with the problem of suffering.

Would you say that in your life you have suffered, that you have experienced *dukkha*?

As a result of your own actions? (That is, have you caused your own *dukkha*?)

As a result of the actions of others? (That is, have they caused your *dukkha*?)

Do you think that people who aim to live a particularly holy life (such as monks) should have to make extra 'promises'? Can you think of any way in which the extra Five Precepts differ from the first five?

What do you think are the likely problems you would meet if you set out to follow the Eightfold Path?

12·THE PILLARS OF ISLAM

The Muslim religion lays down a clear 'everyday' duty for its followers. There are five 'obligations', known as the Pillars of Islam, which must be performed at various times. These are not just beliefs but actions which show belief.

First, it is important to understand what it means to be a Muslim. This is part of a talk on that subject, given by a Muslim, Muhammad Sarwar Rija:

> 66 To begin with let me tell you what Islam literally means. It is an Arabic word. It means submission, obedience, surrender. 99

All five Pillars therefore show the 'submission' of the Muslim to the Will of God.

The First Pillar
The First Pillar (*shahadah*) is making a statement of faith: 'There is no god but God, and Muhammad is His Prophet.' It is by making this statement that one becomes a Muslim.

Muhammad Sarwar Rija explained its importance in his talk:

> 66 Formally, to become a Muslim, to join the universal community of Islam, one proclaims: '*La ila' ha illallah Muhammad ur rasulullah.*' There is no God, no deity, no being worthy of being worshipped except Allah – sometimes it is translated simply, 'There is no god but God' because, after all, Allah is just the Arabic for God – and Muhammad is messenger of Allah. This proclamation must accompany, rather be preceded by, a sincere and heartfelt belief in the two clauses. An utterance without belief is not enough and does not constitute faith. 99

The declaration of faith (or other texts such as the one shown below) are often written up in beautiful handwriting and used for decoration in buildings and on textiles, pottery, brassware and on tiles.

Try making your own copy of the text shown here, and decorating it with a geometric pattern to form a surround for it. (You may be able to use a calligraphy pen or calligraphy felt tip.)

Remember that people and animals are not shown in Islamic art.

'*Truly, the way dearest to God is that of Islam*'

The Second Pillar
The Second Pillar (*salat*) is prayer. The Muslim holy book, the Qu'ran, repeatedly stresses how important it is to pray: 'Make prayers to remember Me'; and 'Prayer at fixed times has been enjoined on the believers'.

Muslims must pray five times a day: between first light and sunrise; just after midday; just after the middle of the afternoon; after sunset; after dark.

Where there is a mosque, a call to prayer will be made from the top of the minaret (see Book 2, unit 18) so that Muslims know the correct times to pray. Traditionally, the call to prayer (*azzan*) is shouted by a man called the *muezzin* or 'caller'. Nowadays, the *azzan* may be tape-recorded and played through an amplifier.

Before prayers can be said, the Muslim must make him or herself clean. The procedure (called *wudu*) not only removes any dirt so the person is not defiled in any way while addressing God but also helps to prepare the mind to concentrate on God.

Men and women usually pray separately. In some Muslim countries, women normally pray only at home. However, a Muslim *can* pray anywhere: at work or school, or even in the street, provided it is a clean place. Wherever he or she is, a Muslim faces Mecca in order to pray. The direction is shown by a niche (*mihrab*) in a mosque. Some Muslims buy a special compass so that they know the direction wherever they are.

Before praying, the Muslim may put down a prayer mat. The prayers are then said (in Arabic). A different posture is taken for each part of the prayer. It begins in a standing position to show that one is listening to God. Then the Muslim bows to show respect to God, then straightens up. Next the Muslim prostrates himself twice, touching the ground with the forehead, knees, nose and palms. Between each prostration, the Muslim sits back on his heels. (Again, particular words are said at that point.) Lastly, one turns one's head to the left and right to say the final prayers. This whole sequence is performed two, three or four times according to the time of day.

On the Muslim holy day, Friday, prayers are said in the Mosque (see Book 2, unit 18).

Muslims also say private, personal prayers in their own language.

The Third, Fourth and Fifth Pillars

The Third Pillar, *zakat* (the act of giving to the less fortunate) is studied in Book 2, unit 25. The Fourth Pillar, *saum* (the act of fasting, especially in the month of Ramadan) is studied in Book 2, unit 24. The Fifth Pillar, *hajj* or pilgrimage, is studied in Book 2, unit 30.

Conclusion

Discuss why each Pillar is important to a Muslim.
Make a table with the headings shown below and then fill in the details for each Pillar.

Pillar number	Islamic and English names	How often it is performed	What it involves	Why it is important

13·THE FIVE Ks OF SIKHISM

Symbols

As you walk along any high street, you will see many symbols or signs which give information without using words. For example, there are road signs: triangular ones giving warnings and round ones giving orders.

Some symbols show ownership. For example, British Rail has its symbol as do many bus companies. Some shops have symbols made out of their initial letters. Symbols can also convey *ideas*. For example, there are those which promise help to the disabled or the deaf, or the idea of friendship suggested by the linked hands of the Commission for Racial Equality.

Make copies of the symbols you can see in your town and note what each represents.

Religious symbols

Each religion has its own symbols. (See Book 1, unit 11.) For example, the symbol of Christianity is the cross while the symbol of Sikhism is the Khanda, the two-edged sword which represents God's concern for truth and justice.

Sikhism also has five other symbols or signs. They came into being when one of the Sikh gurus, Guru Gobind Singh, founded the Khalsa or brotherhood of all Sikhs (see Book 2, unit 23). Each of these symbols says something about the way a Sikh must live his or her daily life and they must be worn by all Sikhs who have joined the Khalsa (unit 10).

Because their names in Punjabi all begin with the letter k, they are known as the five Ks.

Kesh

Kesh is uncut hair. A Sikh must wear his or her hair long, and (in the case of men) beards and moustaches as well. In Sikhism, the human body is thought to be sacred because in it lives a person's spirit. As hair is seen as being an essential part of the body, it must be preserved and never cut off and thrown away. The uncut hair of a Sikh is a symbol of his or her vow to live for God, a vow to dedicate mind and body to God.

The hair must be kept tidy, combed twice a day, washed at least every four days and never dyed.

Kanga

The Kanga is a comb worn to keep the long hair in place under a Sikh's turban. 'Dishevelled hair is not permitted as it is a sign of lethargy, uncleanliness, indifference to responsibility and a cynical attitude towards life.'

Kirpan

The Kirpan is a sword which reminds Sikhs that they are warriors. It is not a weapon for attacking people but one for defending the Sikh faith and protecting the weak and helpless. It is also a sign that a Sikh must have a sword-like mind. Nowadays a Sikh wears only a miniature kirpan or even a very tiny one set into the kanga.

Kaccha (or Kachs)

Kaccha are shorts or underpants worn by men and women as a sign of sexual restraint and to allow easy movement – for example, in battle. (At the time of Guru Gobind Singh, many Indians wore just a loin cloth or *dhoti*. Some holy men wore only a very narrow piece of cloth, called a *langoti*, wound round the loins.)

The kaccha is therefore a sign of modesty and readiness for work.

Kara

The kara is a circular steel bracelet, worn on the right wrist as a reminder that God is one, without beginning or end. The hardness of the steel is a reminder to Sikhs of the need to be strong and the kara is worn by both men and women as a sign that men and women are equal. Its shape is also a reminder of the oneness or unity of the Khalsa.

The Sikh turban

Many people recognise Sikhs by their turbans but the turban is not one of the signs that Guru Gobind Singh told Sikhs they must wear. It is worn by most Sikh men, however, as a way of keeping their long hair clean and tidy and is closely connected with the dignity of a Sikh. It can be any colour but white. Blue and yellow are among the more popular ones.

Younger boys (whose hair is not so long) wear a small handkerchief called a *rumal* to tie up their hair.

Daily life

Those Sikhs who are members of the Khalsa have other duties and obligations, besides accepting the teachings of the gurus and wearing the five Ks. They should:

say prayers every morning and evening
not steal
drink no alcohol nor use tobacco or hemp, etc.
not commit adultery
work honestly
not trust in any magic or charms
treat other Sikhs as brothers and sisters
give to charity
and be ready to sacrifice everything for their faith.

Things to do

1 Design a symbol or badge that shows what you believe in or what you believe is important. If you are a member of a religion, perhaps you can add to the symbol of that religion, to show more precisely what matters especially to you.
2 Discuss what is the value of religious symbols to believers.
3 If possible, invite a Sikh to teach you how to tie a turban.
4 Why were Sikhs distressed when a law was passed in Britain making it compulsory for all motorcyclists to wear crash helmets? Do you think it right that they should now be exempt from this law?
5 Make drawings of the five Ks, and add a sentence to each that a Sikh might say to explain its importance. For example, 'Kesh is important to me because...'

14·THE TEN COMMANDMENTS

To talk about...
Which of these comments do you agree with?

'It would be ever so dull if everyone was good all the time. It changes the routine if someone's bad once in a while.'

'If everyone was good, the world would be a much better place.'

'It's embarrassing if someone is too good and angelic.'

Do you find 'evil' attractive? Is it boring to be good? What do your answers tell you about yourself?

But what would it be like if everyone was free to do as they wished? If we had no rules and just hoped that everyone did the right thing? (Perhaps you have read the book *Lord of the Flies*. What happens there when there are no rules?)

Think back to how the Jews were once slaves in Egypt. There they would have had to do exactly what their Egyptian masters told them to do. Then Moses led them out of Egypt and into freedom.

THE TEN SAYINGS
Once they were away from the harsh disciplines of slavery in Egypt and on their own in the wilderness, the Jews needed a basic set of rules by which to live. The Ten Sayings or Ten Statements (as they are known by Jews) were revealed by God to Moses (see Book 1, unit 15). The Sayings were engraved on two stone slabs or tablets. Moses later broke them when the Israelites worshipped a golden calf but another set was made and kept in the Ark (see Book 2, unit 4).

The Sayings are recorded twice in the Torah (the Five Books of Moses) and, therefore, also in the Old Testament (Exodus 20:1–17 and Deuteronomy 5:6–18).

Look also at Leviticus 11:2–23 and Deuteronomy 14:3–21. In list form, note what the Israelites were and were not allowed to eat.

Which instructions do you think are very sensible when you consider the climate and the fact that the Israelites were wandering in a strange land?

THE TEN COMMANDMENTS
The Ten Commandments were the basis of much of the teaching of Jesus (see unit 15) and have since become the basis of the law of many countries around the world.

To talk about...
1 Do you think there are any of the Commandments that we no longer 'need'?
2 Which ones do you think should be the law of the land as well as being religious rules?
3 In what way is a day off once a week a sign of freedom? Do you think one day a week should be kept different from the rest of the week?

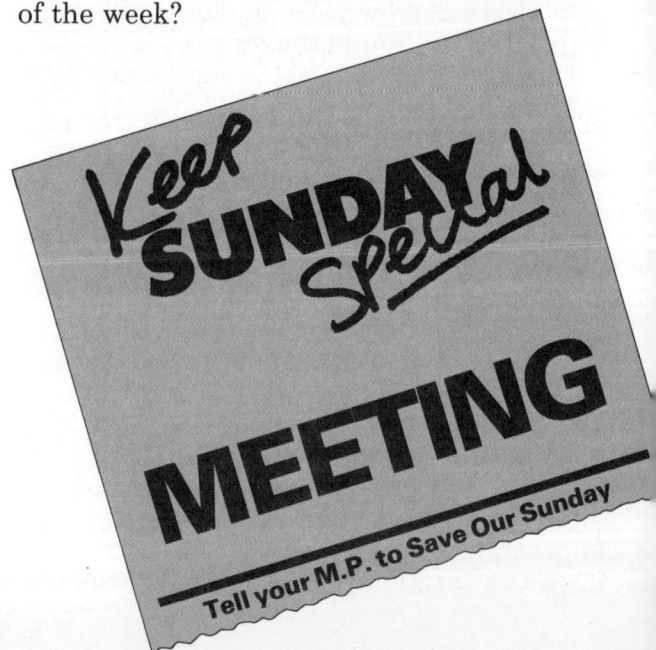
Keep SUNDAY Special
MEETING
Tell your M.P. to Save Our Sunday

4 What is blasphemy? Should it be a crime? Why are many Christians upset when the words 'God', 'Christ' or 'Jesus' are used as swear words?

Some people have questioned whether the Commandments actually date from the time of Moses but most modern scholars now believe they do. One or two of them may, however, have been added to, once the Israelites (as they were then known) had settled in their Promised Land. Which parts do you think might be later additions?

For Jews, the first of the Sayings is verse 6 of the fifth chapter of Deuteronomy. This is not a 'commandment' but is nevertheless the most important of the Sayings. It shows the relationship of the Jewish people to God: He gave them their freedom, they are His people. Verses 7 and 8 together form the second Saying.

The Commandments displayed in a London synagogue

For Jews, the Ten Sayings are not only religious rules. They are the key part of everyday Law. There are, however, many other detailed laws and rules. In particular, they can be found in the Books of Exodus, Leviticus and Deuteronomy. For example,

there are very precise instructions to priests about how to cope with the problem of leprosy. Leviticus 13 and 14 are, for example, a cross between a rulebook and an early medical textbook.

5 What is your duty to your parents? What will it be in thirty or more years' time?
6 Do you think 'Do not commit murder' means more than it says?
7 Find out what Jesus said about committing adultery. (Matthew 5:28.)
8 Is it stealing if you get away with not paying a bus fare?
9 Why is it wrong to make false accusations?
10 What might be a modern version of the last Commandment?
11 Do you think the Commandments make it easier or harder to live one's life?

Write...

1 Write out a version of the Commandments that is particularly relevant to your school.
2 Write out the Commandments in what you think is their order of importance.

ISLAMIC LAW

Like Judaism and Christianity, Islam teaches that people should be obedient to the will of God. Coming after them as it does, it draws on their laws and the Qur'an includes numbers 1 and 5–10 of the Ten Commandments:

> **"** Thy Lord has commanded that you shall not serve any but Him and that you do goodness to your parents....Do not kill your children for fear of poverty.
> And go not nigh to fornication, for it is an indecency....And do not kill anyone whom God has forbidden except for a just cause....Do not say, if people do good to us, we will do good to them, and if people oppress us, we will oppress them, but resolve that if people do good to you, you will do good to them, and if they oppress you, do not oppress them in return.... Repel evil with that which is better. **"**

31

15·THE BEATITUDES

The Sermon on the Mount

The way the world judges what matters and who's important was turned upside down by Jesus.

His teachings are recorded by the writers of all four gospels but his various sayings have been arranged differently by them.

For example, *Luke* seems to have tried to place the teachings in the settings and order in which they occurred.

Matthew arranges his material by topic. For example, he collects together many of the parables in just two of his chapters: 13 and 25.

Matthew also collects together many of the other sayings in chapters 5–7 of his gospel. This section is often referred to as the 'Sermon on the Mount' (see Matthew 5:1 and also Book 2, unit 11). In this 'sermon', Jesus described the characteristics of 'the inhabitants of the kingdom of Heaven'. That is, he said what a person should be like or should do in order to gain entry to the 'kingdom of Heaven'. Some Christians say the 'kingdom of Heaven' means literally 'Heaven' (a life with God after death). Others say Jesus brought the kingdom of Heaven to earth and that it is with us now if we only knew it. If things are not perfect, then that is only because people still do not follow the way of Jesus.

THE BEATITUDES

The Beatitudes are a series of verses within the Sermon on the Mount. In them, Jesus outlined what people must do or how they should live in order to be 'happy'. (The word *beatus* means 'happy' or 'blessed'.)

Some of the sayings are very unexpected and unlike 'what the world says' (see above).

The table opposite shows how they are recorded in Matthew's and Luke's gospels. The sayings have been remembered slightly differently by the two writers and we cannot tell for certain what were Jesus' exact words.

How many Beatitudes are there in each gospel?

What differences can you find? E.g. what kind of poverty is mentioned?

Which are the same in both versions?

NB In his teaching, Jesus never suggested that his followers should allow the poor to suffer simply because they would have their reward later.

The New Commandments

Christians sometimes say that Jesus came to replace or overthrow the Law of Moses. But find Matthew 5:17 and also 5:20. What *did* he say?

On another occasion, when asked which was the most important Commandment, he did give what are known as the 'Two Great Commandments' (see Matthew 22:34–40, Mark 12:28–34 or Luke 10:25–28 and Book 2, unit 12 of this *Course*).

But he did not say that these Commandments replaced the Ten Commandments. Indeed, he gave five examples of how the Ten Commandments should be obeyed.

Look up the following:

Murder (and anger)	Matthew 5:21–22
Adultery	Matthew 5:27–28
Oaths (and swearing)	Matthew 5:33–37
Retaliation	Matthew 5:38–42
Loving others	Matthew 5:43–44.

How easy is it to keep these 'new' Commandments?

Write...

1 Write out a version of the Ten Commandments so that they include the teachings of Jesus.

2 Write a modern version of the Beatitudes which Jesus might have spoken had he been teaching today.

Matthew 5:3–12	Luke 6:20b–23	Luke 6:24–26
3 Blessed are the poor in spirit, for theirs is the kingdom of heaven.	20b Blessed are you poor, for yours is the kingdom of God.	24 But woe to you who are rich, for you have received your consolation.
4 Blessed are those who mourn, for they shall be comforted.		
5 Blessed are the meek, for they shall inherit the earth.		
6 Blessed are those who hunger and thirst for righteousness, for they shall be satisfied.	21 Blessed are you who hunger now, for you shall be satisfied. Blessed are you who weep now, for you shall laugh.	25 Woe to you that are full now, for you shall hunger. Woe to you that laugh now, for you shall mourn and weep.
7 Blessed are the merciful, for they shall obtain mercy.		
8 Blessed are the pure in heart, for they shall see God.		
9 Blessed are the peacemakers, for they shall be called sons of God.		
10 Blessed are those who are persecuted for righteousness' sake, for theirs is the kingdom of heaven.		
11 Blessed are you when men revile you and persecute you and utter all kinds of evil against you falsely on my account.	22 Blessed are you when men hate you and when they exclude you and revile you and cast-out your name as evil on account of the Son of man!	26 Woe to you when all men speak well of you
12 Rejoice and be glad, for your reward is great in heaven for so men persecuted the prophets who were before you.	23 Rejoice in that day, and leap for joy, for behold, your reward is great in heaven, for so their fathers did to the prophets.	for so their fathers did to the false prophets.

Conclusion

Discuss what the main world faiths seem to
have in common in their teachings about
how their members should live their
everyday lives.

16·CHRISTIAN PRAYER

In Book 2, unit 11 of this course we studied some of the teachings of Jesus on the subject of prayer. In his 'Sermon on the Mount', Jesus said to his followers not 'If you pray...' but 'When you pray...'. (See that part of the 'Sermon' which deals with prayer: Matthew 6:5–15.) For Christians, prayer is, therefore, an essential part of their religion.

When Christians pray they are talking to God. They are also meant to listen; to try to empty their minds so as to allow God to speak to them.

For the Christian, prayer is often a group activity (for example, in church). Either one person (often the priest or minister) will say the prayers and the others (the congregation) will listen and think the prayer with him or her; or, with the help of prayer books, they may all join in and say the prayer together.

Prayer is also a private activity. Many Christians say personal prayers on getting up in the morning and before going to bed. Many say a prayer of thankfulness ('grace') before or after each meal.

Sometimes set prayers are used (especially in church services). At other times, the person praying will make up the prayer as he or she goes along, saying what is on his or her mind.

The following passage is taken from a book written to help Christians to pray:

66 If you are really convinced of your belief in God, that He is close to you, closely interested in you; if you really believe that He has set you in the world and brought you so far with a definite purpose, and that you will only make the most of life if you fulfil His purpose, it will be strange if you pray in the morning and again at night but in between give God never a thought.
Remember that to pray it is not necessary (though it may be helpful) to kneel down, to say words, or even in any way to appear to pray;

the recollection of God's constant presence at all sorts of odd moments, the thought of His purpose and protection springing up from time to time during the day, these are Prayer. **99**

Types of prayer

There are many types of Christian prayers, but they are often thought of as belonging to one or other of five types:

Praise in which the Christian talks to God (or thinks about) the greatness of God and His creation.

Thanksgiving in which the Christian thanks God for the good things of life, for the life and example of Jesus and for particular things that have happened.

Penitence in which the Christian owns up to what he or she has done wrong and expresses his or her sorrow. Like the other forms of prayer, this can be either a group or private prayer. When it is part of a church service it is usually known as 'the confession'. Catholics are expected to go to church at other times as well to make a private confession to the priest of all their failings.

Petition in which Christians ask God to help them either generally or in particular matters.

Intercession in which Christians pray for other people and their needs.

Christians believe that God hears all their prayers and answers them in the way that is best. This may of course not be in the way the person praying was hoping for!

Things to do

1 Can you describe any experience of prayer (either helpful or disappointing) that you have had?

2 How would *you* describe prayer?

3 Discuss whether you think it is possible

Sometimes, Christians pray in public as witness of their faith

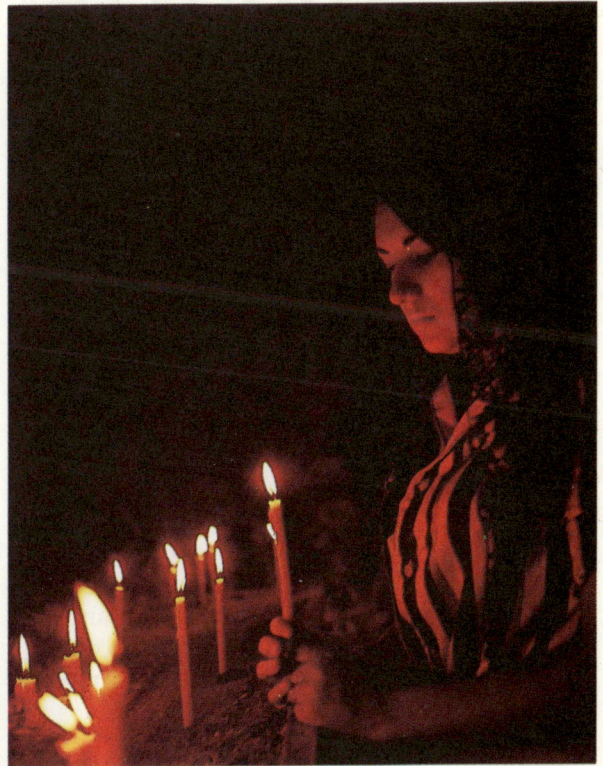

Roman Catholic Christians often light a candle in church as a symbol of their prayer burning on after they have finished saying it

for members of different religions to pray together.

4 Discuss whether prayer should be part of your school assembly.

5 Write a collection of prayers or thoughts that could be suitable for use in your assembly. Is it possible to make them acceptable to all believers and to non-believers? Are they less 'effective' or convincing than the prayers of one particular religion?

17·CHRISTIAN WORSHIP

Christian worship is very varied and can take many different forms. There are not only the Orthodox, Catholic and Protestant traditions but many different styles of worship within each of these traditions.

Christian worship usually takes place in a church (or chapel or cathedral: see Book 2, unit 17). It can take place in the open air, in a simple hall, or a small group of Christians may meet in one of their own homes (such a group being known as a 'house church').

Worship is likely to include both private (or personal) prayer and group (or congregational) prayer. There are also likely to be readings from the Bible and there may be hymn singing and a sermon. Christian worship often takes the form of a service of Holy Communion or the Mass (see Book 2, unit 14).

Quakers

Members of the Society of Friends are often known as Quakers. They have no priests or ministers; they do not sing hymns, have prayer books or sermons. Much of their Meetings for Worship consists of silence, members speaking only when they feel have an important experience or thought they wish to share. Members say such Meetings are 'refreshing', feeling they gain strength and support from the company of other Friends.

Pentecostal Christians

Pentecostal Christian services are often very lively and informal with much spontaneous prayer, singing and chanting. Powerful and moving sermons are often a part of these services. See also Book 1, unit 23.

Salvationists (members of the Salvation Army) also enjoy lively music during their worship

An open-air service of Holy Communion in Africa

Priests and ministers

" For centuries, the three main orders of clergymen within the largest part of the Christian Church have been bishops, priests and deacons.

The priest is the basic order. Clergymen may hold a number of offices and titles (e.g. vicar, curate) but they remain priests. Some Christians have objected to the name 'priest' or the idea of 'priesthood'. They have preferred to call their clergymen by a variety of titles: 'minister', 'pastor', 'presbyter' and 'moderator'.

Behind these different names there are different ideas of what to expect of 'a man of God'.

To 'minister' is to serve: a 'pastor' is someone who feeds and looks after the flock. These titles indicate the kind of work a person does. Priests actually do much the same sort of work, but their title is defined more in terms of what they *are*...

Some people have come to regard the priest as a man set apart from other men, a man 'in holy orders' suspended somewhere between divinity and humanity. In their opinion he should remain aloof and detached from the usual human interests and ambitions, and concentrate on what is strictly religious. He should not marry nor wear ordinary clothes. He should always live and look the special priestly part.

Others saw and see him as a man apart only in the special things he is allowed to do, such as celebrating Holy Communion and conducting church marriages; and also in his special abilities as a preacher of sermons, a personal adviser and an expert in theology. **"**

Peter Watkins and *Erica Hughes*

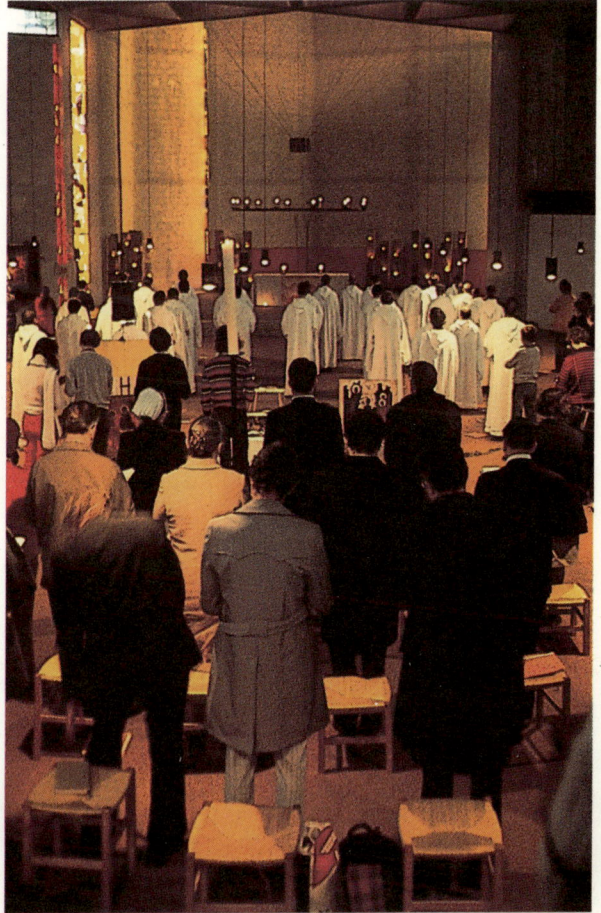

Holy Communion in a modern church in France

2 What arguments can you think of in favour of worship being dignified and having a set order? And what arguments can you think of in favour of lively and spontaneous worship?

3 Can watching a televised church service be 'worship'?

4 Do you think Christians should be proud of the fact that they find it possible to worship God in so many different ways, or would it be better (or more convincing) if Christians all worshipped in the same way?

To talk about...

1 Why do you think many Christians feel a church building should be as beautiful and as impressive as possible? Why do you think others think this is unnecessary?

Project

If possible, invite a member of the clergy to your classroom to talk about worship in his (or her) church and to show you the robes, books and other things used in worship.

18 · MONKS AND NUNS

CHRISTIAN HONKS AND NUNS

Monks and nuns are men and women who choose to devote their whole lives to God. They usually make three vows:

the vow of poverty: to have no possessions of their own

the vow of chastity: to have no sexual relations

the vow of obedience: to obey the will of God and the rules of their 'order' (the group of monks or nuns to which they belong)

Many live apart from the world in communities called monasteries or convents. They spend their time in prayer and study of the Bible; they go to either four or seven services a day (beginning with Matins in the early morning and ending with Compline in the evening); and also work – perhaps gardening or making things to sell in order to earn money to pay for the things the community needs.

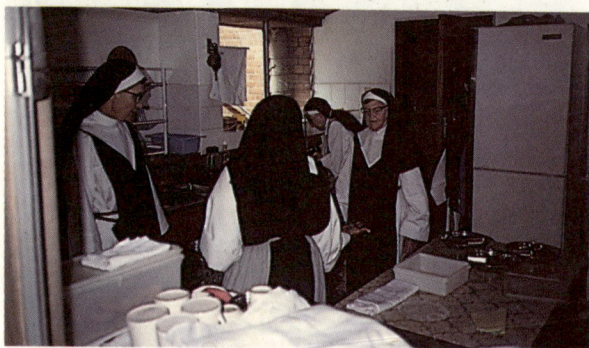

This is part of the story of Ruth Burrows who, while a teenager, began to realise she might perhaps become a nun.

66 Like every Catholic girl at that time, educated at a convent school, I was aware there was such a thing as a 'religious vocation' – that is a calling to serve God as a nun. I knew that, in theory at any rate, this was a highly regarded life; but it was not at all appealing to me. I wanted independence and then marriage.

It was a custom in our school for the girls to make a retreat for a few days. This meant going to a quiet place, perhaps a convent or a special retreat house, and spending time in Bible study, in prayer and at services. Our retreat was to take place during the Whitsun half-term holiday. But, as I said at the time, 'I don't see why I should have to go on their silly old retreat. It's my time, I don't see why those nuns have got the right to make me go.' But I went. I was a nuisance. I refused to be silent at the proper times. I chattered. I pestered others. I didn't listen in chapel to the sermon. But then suddenly, in the middle of the second day, I was seized with fear. A new fear, not like any of the others I had known. What did God think of me? After tea, I went to confession.

Priest (*quietly*): Why have you behaved this way, child?

Ruth (*hesitating*): I was mad with the nuns.

Priest: Why?

Ruth: They're trying to make us pious. They're trying to force us to be religious.

Priest: Are you sure that's the only reason?

Ruth: Yes.

Priest: In your heart, are you sure?

Ruth: Yes, I've said.

Priest: Are you perhaps afraid that God is asking something of you and you don't want to listen?

I knew quite well what he was hinting at. Hinting that perhaps I had a vocation, that God was asking something special of me, and that I was refusing to listen.

When she left school, Ruth Burrows turned down a place she had won at Oxford University to become a member of a very strict order of nuns called the Carmelites. 'God didn't call me to an easy life – but He did call me and so I had to follow. And now I've found happiness and peace. Great happiness and peace.'

Other nuns live 'in the world', working at such jobs as teaching and nursing (like, for example, Mother Teresa in Calcutta).

BUDDHIST MONKS AND NUNS

Just as there are Christian monks and nuns, so there are Buddhist ones. The Buddha himself founded an order known as the *Sangha*. Besides the Precepts (see unit 11), they too must have no sexual relations; must not take what is not given; take no human life; nor pretend to have powers they do not have.

Many stories are told about men keen to become Buddhist monks spending days waiting to be admitted to a monastery.

Monk: Well, you've been kneeling here for three days now. You seem to be fairly serious about it. Why do you want to be a monk? To gain enlightenment I suppose? To spend your life in meditation?

Man: No. In order to help people in need.

Monk: Mm. Well, you may enter. Not as a monk you understand. Not yet. But as a visitor. If your desire to become a monk proves serious, you will be admitted to the Meditation Hall later. Have you brought any possessions? Belongings?

Man: I thought a monk was to have no possessions, except...

Monk: Except his robe, his needle and thread, razor, water strainer and begging bowl. Yes. You're right.

Man: Why the begging bowl? Is not the monastery presented with gifts of food? Why, in the past, even I have given food for the monks...

Monk: Oh yes, we're given food. But if you did not beg, how else would you learn humility?

Buddhist monks do not simply spend their time begging and meditating. They work as teachers (showing people how to dig wells and cultivate crops) and help to build schools and hospitals. In Buddhist countries, boys often spend a period of one to four months living the life of a monk, in a monastery.

To talk about...

1 Is it a 'waste' of life being a monk or nun?

2 What good would it do you to live as a monk or nun for a while? Would you find it easy? (There is a scheme in Britain called 'Give a Year to God' in which older teenagers and young men give up a year of their life to live a monastic life.)

Project

Plan and improvise or write your own play in which a young person decides to become a monk or nun. What do their friends, parents and teachers say?

What else can you find out about the life of a monk or nun? Write a story called 'A Day in the Life of Brother...(*or* Sister...)'.

19·SOCIAL ACTION

Banishing poverty

The scene is a courtroom with judges, lawyers, jury. The accused, Mr/Mrs Poverty, is in the dock, with two police officers, whilst the judge sits on a raised chair.

Judge: The charge reads as follows:

First, that you conspired with governments to cheat and defraud millions of people of their rightful inheritance of good health.

Second, that you, Poverty, conspired with persons unknown to take advantage of millions of workers in both cities and countryside, to exploit and degrade them.

Third, that by wilful neglect you have caused the death of millions of children.

How do you plead – guilty or not guilty?

Prisoner: Not guilty your honour.

Judge: Call the first witness for the prosecution. Please address the court.

Witness 1: My name is Garcia de Silva – I am a doctor in the city of Bahia in North East Brazil. Most of my patients are malnourished – they're ill simply because they are too poor to buy enough food to keep body and soul together. They will never be fit and strong because they are the victims of the accused – Poverty. As far as I am concerned Poverty – this person here – is a killer. Many of my patients are already too ill to be saved – destroyed by this shadowy killer. My government's efforts are undermined by this evil killer. In Brazil we are spending only about £1 a head a year on health compared with more than £50 a head in the UK, and we need twice as many doctors. It's his (her) fault – Poverty is the killer!

Judge: Thank you. (*Pause*) Call the next witness. Please present the jury with your evidence.

Witness 2: Yes, your honour. I can testify to the charge that workers have been exploited and degraded because of him/her – because of Poverty. I work on a sugar cane estate in the Philippines in S.E. Asia. We start cutting the cane at 6 a.m. but even then you can't escape from the sun.

It's blistering hot in the afternoon but cooler by 5 p.m. when we finish. We have to work long hours to avoid getting into the clutches of him/her – (*pointing to Poverty*). When there's no work we live on credit at the company shop to get rice – but I'll never be able to pay off the debts.

We women live a hand to mouth existence. I've only got two dresses – I wear one while the other is in the wash: I can't buy another one because I must get more clothes for the kids. We just pray to God to give us good health because we have no money for medicines. We are kept poor – and when we objected, some of my friends were arrested – others have been beaten up – and who is to blame? Poverty – there in the dock – he's (she's) to blame!

Judge: That will be all. Does the prosecution wish to present any more evidence?

Witness 3: Yes, your honour, I wish to speak for the prosecution.

Judge: Please present your evidence; who are you?

Witness 3: I work for the aid agency, Christian Aid. In my job I have to travel to many parts of the world – it may sound glamorous but members of the jury, I see suffering and poverty that you can never imagine.

There's a saying that a warm man can never understand what it's like to be cold! Well, perhaps you will never understand the misery inflicted by Poverty over there (*pointing*) but the facts speak for themselves. Last year 17

million children died because of poverty –
that's 30 children every minute – and it
will be the same this year. Ninety per
cent of those who died had not been
immunised against six deadly killers. Yet
for just £2.50 a child, this could be done.
£2.50 is the price of a life: or the price of
a seat at the cinema.

I could give much more evidence –
about the thousands of children who
have to work in factories, about those
who cannot afford to go to school. Only
recently we received a letter from the
Philippines saying school classes in one
area had dropped by thirty per cent. The
parents could no longer afford to pay the
tuition fees because the world price of
cooking oil which they produce had
fallen again. That's another generation of
wasted children! Members of the jury,
think carefully – the evidence is here
before you.

Judge: Thank you for your evidence.
Prisoner, do you wish to call evidence for
your defence?

Prisoner: I wish to conduct my own
defence your honour. I cannot deny or
disprove the evidence presented to the
court today but my case is that it is not
my fault. I am not guilty – I am just the
victim of a system which makes people
poor – and then they blame me. Some
governments allow the process of
creating poverty to get out of hand.
Members of the jury, I don't like
spreading poverty – but I just can't help
it – it's the system. Some people just seem
to get richer and many, many others just
get poorer (*beginning to shout at the jury*)
I can't help it, it just seems to happen –
it's out of control...

Judge: Thank you. Please be silent. Ladies
and gentlemen of the jury, you have
weighed the evidence presented by the
witnesses. Now you must decide and
justice must prevail. What is your
verdict?

Christian Aid

So who is guilty? Who or what is to blame?
What *is* your verdict?

In groups, form 'juries' to decide your
answers to these questions.

Can you make any recommendations to
the judge as to what should be done?

Rehearse and present a production of the
scene, and of your own discussions and of
your conclusion to the scene.

The sketch was written to illustrate the
work of the charity Christian Aid and the
work which that organisation sees as being
most necessary in the world today.
Christian Aid's aim is to help to solve the
inequalities in the world by working to
prevent disease, hunger and injustice;
and by providing money, materials and
knowledge to help those in need.

Christian Aid is one way Christians have
tried obey the commandment, 'Love thy
neighbour'.

Other religions have their charities and
organisations that exist to help those in
need. For example, the Central British
Fund for World Jewish Relief helps victims
of discrimination and racism.

Projects

1 Write an article that could (or should?)
appear in a newspaper during Christian Aid
Week (the third week in May) to remind
people in this country of their social
responsibilities. Or perhaps you could write
a letter to your local paper, expressing
what you feel about this topic.

2 Compile a wall display (or montage)
called 'Work Outstanding' which shows
what still needs to be done in the world
and what the various charities are doing to
solve the problems. You could use cuttings
from newspapers, colour supplements and
advertising material from the charities, as
well as your own poems, articles and art
work. You might be able to arrange to
display this project in your school or in a
shop in your nearest town centre during
Christian Aid Week.

20 · PREACHING THE FAITH

AMOS

Amos lived about 750BCE, a hundred years after Elijah (see Book 2, unit 9). His home was at Tekoa, south of Bethlehem in the southern kingdom of Judah. He was a shepherd who also looked after some fig trees (or, according to some versions of the Bible, sycamore trees). He sold the wool from the sheep in the much richer towns of the northern kingdom, Israel. For fifty years, there had been peace and prosperity in that area. Businesses thrived, fortunes were made – and the rich led decadent lives. On his trips to the north, Amos felt he must preach against all that he saw was wrong in Israel.

Amos: You people of Israel have sinned again and again. Even for the cost of a pair of sandals, you'll sell a man into slavery. You trample on the weak, you're sexually immoral and, in the temple, you drink wine taken from those who owe you money!

Amos felt his message was given to him by God, and he felt this so strongly he just had to stand up and preach.

Amos: ...and I tell you this, God will destroy your holy places, yes, He will destroy your temples. And why? Because your religion is false. Oh yes, your temples are decorated prettily enough, you've built fine altars, but you're not meant to worship an altar! You should worship God Himself! And secondly. Many of you have got rich by exploiting the poor. And what do you do with your wealth? You build yourselves second homes out in the countryside when the poor have nowhere to live! I tell you, when the time comes, God will destroy every large house in the country! And lastly, you women of Samaria, you rich women here in this capital city, you grow fat like well-fed cows! You send your husbands out to work, to oppress the poor, to get rich so they can keep you provided with alcohol so you can drink your afternoons away. I tell you, the day will come when you'll be dragged outside the city wall and left to die.

All of you, just because things go well at the moment, because you live in comfort, you think you can do as you please, but the day will come, I tell you, when your land will be over-run and you'll be destroyed...

He was the first prophet whose message was written down in any detail. The book Amos in the Jewish Tenakh (the Old Testament) includes, besides his sermons, descriptions of a series of visions he had. See Amos 7:1–9; and 8:1–14.

Not surprisingly, Amos was very unpopular. He was right however. Some thirty years later, the land of Israel was invaded by Assyrians, the capital was destroyed and many of the people were sent into exile.

To talk about...

1 Can you think of any present day prophets: people who (like Amos) are prepared to stand up and to say what they think is right, even if it is unpopular?
2 What would you say to the suggestion that such preachers are simply 'kill-joys'? Can you defend them against such a charge?
3 If you had the courage, what things would you preach against? Unemployment? Sex outside marriage? Drug abuse?
4 In the Middle Ages, the Christian Church tried to keep people from sinning by preaching about the Seven Deadly Sins: gluttony, greed, lechery, sloth (or laziness), pride, anger and envy. What do you think

are the Seven Deadly Sins of today? (Or have they remained the same?)

Preach about...
Plan and give your own sermon on the subject, 'I don't think it's right that...' (To be really successful at this, you should be able to change your listeners' minds about your subject!)

GANDHI
Another great preacher who set out to change society because of his religious beliefs was Mohandas Gandhi. He was a Hindu, born in India in 1869, and his aim throughout life was to seek and to teach the truth.

As a young man, he went to London to study law and then worked in South Africa, where he was badly treated because of his colour. He wanted to improve conditions there for non-whites, but only by non-violent means. He spoke and preached on many occasions and gained many followers. When new laws were introduced by the white government which meant that people had to sign certain papers before they could travel around the country, Gandhi persuaded the people simply not to sign. Eventually the government had to change its mind.

Gandhi returned to India which, at that time, was part of the British Empire. He believed Indians should rule themselves, rather than be governed by another country. He spoke about this at many, many meetings and became a popular leader. He still preached non-violence. Indeed, throughout his life, he refused to kill any living thing. He was, for example, a strict vegetarian.

As he became more and more popular, it was not surprising that the British tried to stop him from preaching. He was put in prison several times but his teaching became more and more popular and eventually India was given its independence in 1947. Sadly, the Hindus and Muslims in India found it impossible to work together and so the country was divided into Hindu India and Muslim Pakistan (which included what is now Bangladesh).

Tragically, for a man who had preached non-violence all his life, Gandhi was assassinated by a young man early in 1948.

He is remembered as a great political leader, but also as a man whose beliefs were founded on his religion. He did, however, believe that the caste system (see unit 7) was a 'blot' on Hinduism and did much to try to end it.

Gandhi was known as Mahatma ('the Great Soul') Gandhi.

Conclusions
1 Why do you think some people feel they must become preachers?
2 How else do people express their religious beliefs? Write brief notes to summarise the main points from these five units. You might arrange the points in two columns, showing how (a) people express their relationship with God and (b) their obligations to their neighbours.

21·LOVE AND MARRIAGE

To talk about...

What do you think will determine who you marry?

    The person's looks?

    Their character?

    Their money?

    A feeling that you love each other?

    Your parents' advice?

    Because there's nobody else?

When do you think you will marry?

    In your teens?

    Twenties? Or thirties?

    When you've got your own home? Never?

How many children will you want?

    One? Two? More?

    None?

    Will you adopt or foster if you can't have any of your own?

The one that you marry...

What do you expect about the person you might marry? Draw or trace the table below and fill it in to show what you look for or hope for in your future partner.

Civil marriage

For most people who have a religious faith, getting married is a religious occasion. It is celebrated in particular ways, according to the customs of the different religions – as we shall see in the following units.

In this country, there are many people who do not go to church or any other religious meeting place who still like the idea of being married in church. There are, however, many who choose to be married in a register office, where the ceremony is conducted by the local registrar (an official who keeps records of all births, marriages and deaths).

To marry, you must be: not married already, able to understand the ceremony and give your consent, and not be a close relative of the person you are marrying. There must be two witnesses aged 16 or over present at the ceremony. You can marry from the age of 18 upwards or (provided you have your parents' or guardians' consent) from the age of 16. The law sees marriage as a *contract*: a binding agreement between two people to share their lives and property, with rights and duties on both sides.

Many people who are married at a register office still choose to make the ceremony an impressive and memorable occasion by wearing special clothes (a bride's white wedding dress being a sign

He or she will have	the same	different	doesn't matter	to change	you will change
Race					
Politics					
Religion					
Hobbies/ interests					
Personal qualities (e.g. patience, humour, quick temper...)					

or symbol of purity) and by travelling in decorated cars. The bride usually carries a bouquet of flowers. Following the ceremony at the register office, there is a reception (a special meal or party at which the wedding cake is cut and speeches are made). The whole event is normally recorded with many photographs or perhaps on video and is reported in the local newspaper. Relatives and friends send cards and presents to the couple.

To talk about...

1 What do you think are the most important reasons for getting married?
2 Is it wrong to be married in church or in any other type of religious ceremony if you are not a believer?
3 What are your reactions to this dialogue from a play?

David Hargreaves and Nicola Burridge are engaged and planning for their marriage and first home. Nicola's mother, Jane (who is divorced) is very disappointed to hear that David and Nicola do not intend to get married in church.

Nicola: There's not going to be any pink satin or maids of honour. Nothing like that. No fuss. No panic. Ten minutes in and out at the Town Hall. That's what we agreed.
Jane: Who agreed? I don't remember being consulted.
Nicola: David and me. It's our wedding.
David: And I'm not poncing about in church for anyone.
Jane: A church wedding can be a simple affair.

Nicola: It would be a lie, Mum. We don't believe all that religious stuff.
Jane: It's the promises you make to each other that matter. They wouldn't be a lie, I hope.
Nicola: We can make them just as well at the register office.
Jane: But there wouldn't be any...sense of occasion. A wedding should be solemn.
David: I thought it was supposed to be a celebration.
Jane: Well, dignified then. It means so much. Everything about the service means something. The ring...an unbroken circle, stands for your love going on for ever...
Nicola: Mum...you're beginning to sound like 'True Romances'.
Jane: The white dress stands for purity...
Nicola: I'm not wearing a white dress and getting married in church to prove to the neighbours I've been a good girl!

Marianne Cook

Drama

In threes, develop the scene in an improvisation in which the trio tries to make their wedding plans.

Write...

Have you ever been to a wedding? What sort of wedding was it? Did anything take place that surprised you?

Write a description of a wedding.

22·HINDU AND SIKH MARRIAGES

> Europeans think marriage is a private matter between two individuals marrying for love, but Hindus, Sikhs and many other people from Asia and Africa regard it differently. In these communities a marriage concerns two whole families, not just two people, and it demands much careful thought.
>
> *W. Owen Cole*

HINDU MARRIAGES

> Marriages are arranged for a boy and girl by their parents, and until recently the choice of partners was severely restricted by caste.
>
> In the past, some Hindu families considered it so important to get their daughters married to good husbands that they arranged marriages for them at a very early age – even four or five – and paid large dowries to the bridegroom's family. In 1955 the minimum age for marriage was fixed by the law of the Republic of India at eighteen for boys and fifteen for girls, and the dowry system is now banned, though some families get round the law.
>
> *A Handbook on Hinduism*

A Hindu wedding

Before the ceremony, the bride will prepare herself carefully. She will have bathed and her mother, sisters and girlfriends will have rubbed ointment into her skin and helped her to apply special make-up to her eyes, forehead, hands and feet. On her forehead she will wear the *tilaka*, the red spot worn by Hindu women to show that they are blessed. She will wear a red *sari*, decorated with gold.

The wedding ceremony is often held in a courtyard at the bride's house or in a convenient nearby street, square or park. The groom arrives (traditionally on horseback), his face veiled with threads of beads or flowers, and accompanied by his family and friends and sometimes even a band. The two families exchange presents.

The ceremony itself is performed under a canopy, in front of a priest. A fire is lit to show the presence of God. Hymns are said or sung and then the bride's parents give her to her husband by placing her hands in his. The bride's brothers then pour fried rice over her hands as a sign they approve of the marriage. (Rice, rather than confetti, used to be thrown at western weddings.)

The most important part of the ceremony then follows. The bride's sari and the groom's *kurta* (a long shirt) are tied together. They then walk round the fire together seven times, making their promises to each other: to be loyal, faithful, to look after each other, etc. They end by saying together, 'Into my will, I take your heart; your mind shall follow mine. Let your heart be mine and mine be yours.'

The ceremony is followed by feasting, music and dancing.

THE SIKH MARRIAGE CEREMONY

> Because of the social and domestic eminence accorded to the parents, it is regarded as a duty for them to arrange for and actively contribute towards the marriage of their offspring. Sometimes, the marriage is arranged without the couple having met one another and the nuptials are performed on the faith of the choice of the respective parents. However, in modern times, and particularly out of the area of the villages, a meeting between the pair is arranged and their individual agreement to the marriage is sought. In some families, Western influence has had a large

impact. Young people are allowed to choose their own partners, but it is still deemed necessary to obtain the consent of the parents.

The marriage need not necessarily take place at the Gurdwara (Sikh Temple), but it may be conducted at the bride's home or any other suitable place where the Guru Granth Sahib has been duly installed in the proper manner. Any good Sikh (man or woman) may officiate at the ceremony and, usually, a respected and learned person is chosen.

The officiating person, having ascertained that the parties are Sikhs and that the couple have unequivocally agreed to be married, asks the couple and their parents to stand while the rest of the congregation remains seated. He then prays to God Almighty, invoking His blessing for the proposed marriage and begging His grace on the union of the couple. A hymn is then sung.

The officiant then gives a speech addressed particularly to the couple, explaining the significance of the Sikh marriage: 'The Sikh Gurus had a very high regard for the state of marriage, and they themselves entered into matrimony. They insisted that marriage is not merely a civil or social contract, but that its highest and most ideal purpose is to fuse two souls into one so that they may become spiritually inseparable. Because the Sikh Gurus believed in the equality of women with men, they enjoined that women also should be taught a sound knowledge of their religion, so that by having common religious knowledge, the couple would be better able to cultivate the same basic aims in life and thus achieve harmony of outlook.'

Mrs P. M. Wylam

Hindu wedding

Things to do

1 Hindus say they 'marry, then fall in love'. Why then do you think Asian marriages are usually very stable?
2 Discuss and then list the advantages and disadvantages of arranged marriages.
3 What is meant by 'an extended family'? Discuss (and list) their advantages and disadvantages.
4 Suppose you have been to a Hindu or Sikh wedding. Write a letter to a friend in which you give your account of what happened.
5 If possible, paint a picture which shows the colour and festivity of a Hindu or Sikh wedding.

Sikh wedding

23·KIDDUSHIN: THE JEWISH WEDDING CEREMONY

Kiddushin means 'making holy' and is the name given to the Jewish wedding ceremony. It is very definitely a religious event and normally takes place in the synagogue.

" Many Jewish wedding customs are very much like the wedding customs of non-Jews. One thing that marks a Jewish wedding apart is the *hupah*, or canopy, under which the bridal couple stand during the ceremony.

The hupah is made of white silk or similar material hung like a small ceiling from four poles. It is often embroidered with a saying from the Bible.

The hupah reminds us of many things. In Bible days, the bridal couple were led to a specially prepared tent to spend their wedding night. The hupah may stand for that tent. It may also stand for the *Tallit* with which a groom used to cover his bride. In ancient days the Tallit was a full cape, not a scarf. When someone took another person under his cape, he was offering his protection. So when a groom put his Tallit around his bride, he took her under his protection. Today, he leads her under the hupah to show that he is responsible for her according to God's law.

Standing with the marriage couple at the ceremony are a best man and a maid or matron of honor.

The ceremony itself begins with the rabbi reciting the blessing of the betrothal over a cup of wine. He gives the bridegroom a sip from the cup, then the bride. Then the groom places the wedding ring on his bride's finger, and recites the betrothal pledge: 'Behold, thou art consecrated unto me by this ring, according to the laws of Moses and Israel.'

After the ceremony of the ring, the rabbi reads the *ketubah*, or marriage contract. The ketubah is written in Aramaic, the everyday language of the Jews two thousand years ago. It gives the date, the place, the names of the bride and groom. It says that the groom asked for the bride's hand and was accepted – the contract cannot be made if the bride does not willingly accept the groom. It lists the amount of money that the groom would have to pay if there is ever a divorce. "

The ketubah is signed by the groom and given to the bride: it is now her proof of marriage. Nowadays some Jewish women also sign a ketubah and hand it to their husband.

" After the reading of the ketubah, the marriage ceremony proper begins. It opens with the recitation of seven blessings, which end with praise of God 'who has created joy and gladness, bridegroom and bride, love and brotherhood, pleasure and delight, peace and harmony.'

Both bride and groom then drink from the same cup of wine. There may be a final prayer or blessing. Then a glass is placed on the floor, and the groom crushes it under his foot. The wedding is over and the guests will probably cry out: *Mazal Tov*! Good luck!

Many reasons are given for the custom of smashing the glass. Some scholars say it has to do with the ancient belief that this will keep evil spirits away. A religious reason is that it reminds us of the destruction of the Temple in Jerusalem. Even on the most joyous occasions we must remember that life includes sorrows.

With the ceremony over, the wedding feast begins – with music and dancing and the giving of gifts. "

Harry Gersh

To talk about...

1 Jews have traditionally always married someone of their own race (though it is said thirty per cent of British Jews do not). What are the arguments in favour of this?
2 All Jews are expected to marry and to have children ('Be fruitful and multiply'). Do you think a religion should tell its followers whether or not they should have children?
3 Is it 'wrong' or unnatural to want to remain single?

Things to do

1 In picture strip form, illustrate the stages of a Jewish wedding ceremony.
2 Suppose other religions had their equivalent of a ketubah or marriage contract. Write out how they might be worded in one or two other faiths.

When you are married...

When you are married, who will...

	HIM	HER	BOTH
earn the money			
do the shopping			
cook			
wash up			
look after the car			
do the garden			
get up in the night when the baby cries			
put the children to bed			
decide about holidays			

What do your answers say about you (and about your expectations)?

NORTH WESTERN REFORM SYNAGOGUE
LONDON

ON , the , 57
corresponding to the , 19
the bridegroom
said to the bride
Be thou my wife according to the Law of MOSES *and of* ISRAEL. *I will cherish and honour and maintain thee in truth and faithfulness as it becometh a Jewish husband to do;*
AND the bride assented to the bridegroom's proposal and agreed to be his wife according to the Law of MOSES and ISRAEL, and to cherish and honour her husband as beseemeth a daughter in Israel:
ACCORDINGLY they entered into this holy covenant of love and comradeship, of peace and harmony, to establish a house in Israel to the glory of the Holy and Blessed ONE, who sanctifieth HIS people ISRAEL through the sacred covenant of marriage.
THIS COVENANT was duly executed, signed and witnessed this day.

ק״ק שערי צדק

בשבת
לחדש
שנת חמשת אלפים ושבע מאות
לבריאת עלם למנין שאנו מונים

פה ב אמר ר
היי לי לאשה כדת
משה וישראל ואני אוקיר ואכבד ואפרנס אותך כדרך
בני ישראל המוקירים ומכבדים ומפרנסים את נשיהם
באמונה.

הכלה
החתן
והסכימה מרת
לדברי ר
וקבלה עליה להיות לו לאשה כדת משה וישראל
ולהוקירו ולכבדו כדרך בנות ישראל. על כן כרתו
שניהם ברית אהבה ואחוה ברית שלום ורעת לבנות
בית בישראל לכבוד הקדוש ברוך הוא המקדש עמו
ישראל על ידי חפה וקדושין. כן נעשה בפנינו והכל
שריר וקים.

חתן ש
כלה ש

49

24·MARRIAGE IN THE ANGLICAN CHURCH

There are some differences in the ways in which the various branches of Christianity celebrate marriage. For example, at a Roman Catholic wedding, it is not the priest but the couple who admininster the vows to each other. In some Orthodox churches, the couple make a circular procession round the church to show that marriage has no end. They may also wear crowns to show their importance to one another.

In this unit, we study the marriage service of the Anglican Church (which includes the Church of England). The text is taken from a Church pamphlet:

GETTING MARRIED IN CHURCH

Those who are practising church members feel strongly that they want to make the promises about loving and caring for their partner in the sight of God and with God's blessing. And there are many other people whose idea of God might be less clear, but who still feel that a church is the right place to make such solemn promises.

The Promises

The promises are very ancient and very familiar. Almost certainly they date from before the Norman Conquest in 1066, and they have changed very little. Eight hundred years ago or more, men and women were promising 'to have and to hold, for fairer, for fouler, for better, for worse, for richer, for poorer, in sickness and in health, from this time forward till death do us part'. The man added 'gold and silver I give thee, and with my body I thee worship, and with all my worldly goods I thee honour'; while the woman promised to be 'blithe and obedient in bed and at board'.

The Marriage

In the early centuries of English Christian history the vows were exchanged and the marriage took place at the church door. Then the couple went inside for a nuptial mass and the blessing. It is since the time of the Reformation that marriages have taken place inside the church.

Only in recent years have civil weddings in register offices become common. But the Church of England has always recognised civil weddings as true marriages because, in the marriage ceremony, it is the couple themselves who marry each other by the promises which they make to each other.

In a church wedding the priest pronounces God's blessing on their union, and the congregation prays for the couple and their future life together.

The Church still holds with conviction to Christ's teaching that marriage is a life-long commitment, but it also has a loving concern for those who have tried and failed, and honestly want to try again.

The Service

The couple traditionally arrive separately. The bridegroom comes first with his 'best man', and he and his family and friends usually sit on the right-hand side of the church. The bride's family and friends sit on the left. The bride enters on the arm of a close relation, usually her father, with whom she processes through the church to join the bridegroom and the best man at the chancel steps.

The priest prays for the couple and declares the purposes of marriage. He then asks, as the law requires him to do, if anyone present knows any reason why the marriage should not take place.

Then come the questions to the couple:

> The priest says to the bridegroom:
> > N, will you take N to be your wife?
> > Will you love her, comfort her, honour
> > and protect her, and, forsaking all
> > others, be faithful to her as long as you
> > both shall live?
> He answers:
> > I Will.
> The priest says to the bride:
> > N, will you take N to be your husband?
> > Will you love him, comfort him, honour
> > and protect him, and, forsaking all
> > others, be faithful to him as long as
> > you both shall live?
> She answers:
> > I will.

The priest may receive the bride from the hands of her father.
The bride and bridegroom face each other.
The bridegroom takes the bride's right hand in his, and says:

> > I, N, take you, N,
> > to be my wife,
> > to have and to hold
> > from this day forward;
> > for better, for worse,
> > for richer, for poorer,
> > in sickness and in health,
> > * to love and to cherish,
> > till death us do part,
> > according to God's holy law;
> > and this is my solemn vow.
> They loose hands.

The bride takes the bridegroom's right hand in hers, and says:

> > I, N, take you, N,
> > to be my husband,
> > to have and to hold
> > from this day forward;
> > for better, for worse,
> > for richer, for poorer,
> > in sickness and in health,
> > § to love and to cherish,
> > till death us do part,
> > according to God's holy law;
> > and this is my solemn vow.

* This line may be altered to: 'to love, cherish and worship'
§ This line may be altered to: 'to love, cherish and obey'

They complete their promises by the giving and receiving of the wedding ring, or by an exchange of rings. The priest declares them to be 'man and wife, in the name of the Father and of the Son and of the Holy Spirit', and pronounces God's blessing on them. Then all the congregation pray for the couple, asking God's help for them as they begin their new life together.

To talk about...

1 What do you think of the traditional marriage promises? Would you be prepared to make them?
2 In the modern service, would you be prepared to include the words 'worship' and 'obey'? Do you agree that the bride and groom should make different promises?
3 What do you think marriage is for? In what order of importance would you put the reasons given by the Chruch of England? What other reasons might you include?

Project

Collect reports of weddings from your local newspaper. What do the weddings have in common?

What are the duties of each of the main people involved? For example, the best man, the bride's father, ushers, etc.

25·TILL DEATH US DO PART?

DIVORCE

Despite the promises made at a wedding, not every marriage lasts. It may end simply with a 'separation'; with the still-married couple living apart. The legal ending of a marriage is called *divorce*. Divorce is commoner in western society than elsewhere but up to about a hundred years ago it was comparatively rare in the west as well. Gradually, however, people in the west have come to think it better that a marriage should break up than that a really unhappy couple should stay together. At present in Britain, there is one divorce for every three or four marriages. In parts of America, there is one divorce for every two marriages.

Marriages break down for a variety of reasons. The couple might find that they have gradually grown apart, and now share fewer interests and friends. It may be because of rows about money or drink, or it may be a result of stress from worries such as unemployment. One partner may have fallen in love with someone else. Rarely is there one single reason.

Quite often, parents find it a very difficult subject to talk about to their children – yet the split is between the parents and only very rarely between a parent and the children. Nevertheless, it can leave the children with very mixed feelings: anger, embarrassment, fear, guilt, relief, shock, sorrow, surprise.

The different world faiths have varying attitudes to divorce:

Hinduism	Orthodox Hinduism does not allow divorce
Buddhism	Does occur among Chinese Buddhists but is very rare

Judaism	Allowed (even encouraged) if the marriage has broken down but is nevertheless rare
Christianity	**Roman Catholics:** not allowed but the Church will 'annul' (= 'make nothing') marriages which have not been 'fulfilled' or which were not legally made **Orthodox Christianity:** allowed 'in cases of extreme distress' **Protestant churches:** while upholding the ideal of lifelong marriage, several churches allow divorce
Islam	A man is permitted to divorce his wife 'only as a last resort'; a woman must persuade a court that her husband has 'not acted as a husband'
Sikhism	Allowed but rare

The different Christian attitudes to divorce and re-marriage can be illustrated by these statements from two clergymen:

'I do believe that the promises one takes at marriage mean precisely what they say; that if you say, "till death us do part" or "as long as you shall live", it means precisely that. It is God who marries the couple. Only God can separate them.'

'When people really recognise that something has gone wrong, that the marriage has fallen apart *and* when there's a genuine desire to make a fresh start and seek God's blessing, then it's possible to be re-married in church in a Christian marriage service.'

To talk about...

1 With which of the two clergymen do you agree? Do you think a couple should stay together whatever happens? Or do you believe separation is a good idea if the marriage has really broken down? What about divorce and re-marriage? Does it make any difference if there are children?

2 Why do you think children might experience each of the feelings listed on page 52.

3 Do you think the breakdown of a marriage is usually someone's 'fault' or do you think in some cases 'it just can't be helped'?

4 Do you think a religious faith helps to keep a married couple together?

5 Does a religion which allows divorce set too low a standard?

6 If you believe in divorce, should you take vows to be married 'till death us do part' or 'as long as we shall live'?

7 A hundred years ago there were hardly any divorces. People felt a wife should stay with her husband even if she was very unhappy. Do you think the change is for the better? Is it possible to say which creates the more misery: an unhappy marriage or a divorce? What are the arguments for maintaining a marriage at all costs?

8 In two-thirds of divorces children under the age of sixteen are involved. What opinions and feelings does this fact bring to mind?

Divorce in Islam

Muslim marriages are usually much more stable than Western ones and divorce (although allowed) is rare. This sometimes surprises non-Muslims, especially as Muslim marriages are usually 'arranged' by the couple's parents.

This is because (it is said) parents really know their children and are more likely to make a wise choice as to who will make the best partner for their son or daughter over the long term.

What do you feel about arranged marriages?

Write...

What makes for a happy family? Either write ten commandments that will maintain happy family life or write five sentences each beginning, 'Blessed is the family which ...'

Things to do

1 Revise what we have noted about the place of women in Sikhism (in units 2, 10 and 13 of this book). Write a paragraph about the place of women in Sikhism.

2 Revise what we have noted during this *Course* about Judaism – especially in unit 16 of Book 2. Write a paragraph describing the place of women in the Jewish home and synagogue.

3 Discuss how you think women are regarded in Christianity.

Conclusions

1 What are people doing when they get married? What is a marriage *for*?

2 If two young people make private promises to each other, then why is that not a marriage?

Sometimes children can be the most affected by divorce

26·THE PROBLEM OF SUFFERING

Belsen

On 19 April 1945, the BBC reporter Richard Dimbleby sent this report from Belsen:

66 I picked my way over corpse after corpse in the gloom, until I heard one voice raised above the gentle undulating moaning. I found a girl, she was a living skeleton, impossible to gauge her age for she had practically no hair left, and her face was only a yellow parchment sheet with two holes in it for eyes. She was stretching out her stick of an arm and gasping something, it was, 'English, English, medicine, medicine', and she was trying to cry but she hadn't enough strength. And beyond her down the passage and in the hut there were the convulsive movements of dying people too weak to raise themselves from the floor ...

One woman, distraught to the point of madness, flung herself at a British soldier who was on guard at the camp on the night that it was reached by the 11th Armoured Division; she begged him to give her some milk for the tiny baby she held in her arms. She laid the mite on the ground and threw herself at the sentry's feet and kissed his boots. And when, in his distress, he asked her to get up, she put the baby in his arms and ran off crying that she would find milk for it because there was no milk in her breast. And when the soldier opened the bundle of rags to look at the child, he found that it had been dead for days. 99

Aberfan

Aberfan

In the Welsh mining village of Aberfan, one October morning in 1966, a man-made tip of slurry and other waste material from a coal-mine slid down the mountainside and buried the village primary school. The final death toll was 116 children and 28 adults.

Bangladesh

It was the middle of the night, and Abdul Hadi and his family were sound asleep. Outside their tin-roofed hut on the tiny island of Urir Char, off the coast of Bangladesh, gale-force winds and heavy rain lashed the landscape. All at once a wall of water more than 12 feet high slammed into the building. Hadi grabbed a pair of logs, put them under his armpits and caught hold of two of his young sons. The surf swept them more than three miles out to sea and then miraculously brought them back to land again. The three survived, but Hadi's wife and four other children were lost. He eventually found a daughter's body in a pond. Five days later, Hadi was lining up at a relief center for biscuits and water – and material to build a new home. 'Where else can I go?' he said. 'What Allah has done is done.'

For many people in Bangladesh, that sort of stoicism was the only possible response to the cyclone that subsided early last week after ravaging their country. Relief officials toting up the damage from the storm and deadly tidal bores that had hit over the weekend estimated that at least 10,000 people had been killed and more than 250,000 left homeless. Those figures were mostly the result of guesswork, however, and some observers believed that the actual body count was possibly higher. In 1970 a cyclone that struck the country killed somewhere between 300,000 and 1 million people, one of the worst natural disasters of modern times. *Newsweek* (10 June 1985)

It can be seen therefore that there are three types of suffering:

1 Suffering caused by our inhumanity to others (resulting from greed, desire for power, cruelty, thoughtlessness, etc.).

2 Suffering caused by human incompetence (such as our failure to perfect a drug, our failure to realise a river is prone to flood a particular valley or that a mountain is volcanic, or our carelessness in controlling inventions such as the motor car).

3 Suffering which is 'natural' and apparently unavoidable (such as the typhoon, the famine that results from bad weather, the deformity which afflicts a child from birth, the accident that does not stem from human error or the illness which has no known cause).

Project

Collect newspaper cuttings and photographs from magazines, etc. that show the three types of suffering. Arrange them as three separate wall displays.

The problem

Surely, the argument goes, if God existed and if He were all-powerful and if He loved his creatures, then He would not allow them to kill each other in world wars and would certainly not attack them with plagues and earthquakes and famine. Does the existence of pain and suffering therefore mean that there is no God? Or does it mean He is unloving and uncaring?

Survivors of the Bangladesh tidal wave

So often, these basic questions form an insurmountable barrier to religious belief.

ANSWERS

For a start, all religions teach that it is wrong to inflict suffering on others. They also teach that we should use the gifts we have been given (e.g. medical and other knowledge) to prevent unnecessary suffering.

Hinduism

The basic answer of Hinduism to the problem lies in the law of *karma*: that we are rewarded or suffer in one life because of our actions in a previous one. (See Book 2, unit 29.) For the Hindu, death can be something to look forward to because it is a step towards a new life and eventual 'fusion' with God.

Buddhism

The Buddhist faith is built on the question of why there is suffering. See Book 1, unit 12 of this *Course* and also unit 11 of this book.

Islam

In Islam, suffering serves two purposes. First, it is a direct punishment for sin; secondly, it is a form of test. Through suffering, people are tested to see if they will remain faithful.

Muslims also believe that, were God not merciful, there would be very much more suffering (because we are so very sinful).

To talk about...

1 Is most of the suffering in the world man-made?

2 Do you believe suffering is inevitable?

3 Would life be impossibly dull without suffering? (Would we know when we were happy?) Suppose there were no risks in life?

4 Do you think we have a right not to suffer?

5 What acts might you perform this coming week that would help to lessen someone's loneliness, misery or other suffering?

27·NO EASY ANSWERS

JUDAISM

Why should apparently innocent people suffer? The Jewish Bible (the Tenakh) contains a book which sets out to answer this question. It is the fictional Book of Job.

Job

Job worshipped God. He did no wrong. He helped the poor and sick and gave help to anyone in need. He was humble, and faithful to God.

Then a series of catastrophes happened to Job. His oxen and camels were killed. His sheep were struck by lightning. His sons and daughters were killed when the house they were in was struck by a whirlwind. But Job still trusted in God.

Job: I was born with nothing and I will die with nothing. The Lord gave and now he has taken away. Blessed be the name of the Lord.

Job then became ill: his body was covered with sores, like boils. Still he said nothing against God.

Job: When God sends us something good, we welcome it. How can we complain when He sends us trouble?

Eventually in his continued suffering, Job cursed the day he was born.

Job: I wish I'd died in my mother's womb or died the moment I was born! Why did I live to suffer?

Three of his friends offered possible answers. First, Eliphaz who believed that Job must have done wrong because only the wicked suffer, and that he must accept his punishment because he must have been wicked in the past.

Eliphaz: I have seen people plough fields of evil and sow wickedness like seed. Like a storm, God destroys them in His anger! Happy is the person whom God corrects! Don't resent it when He rebukes you!

The second friend, Bildad, believed God would put things right in the end, and Job must just be patient.

Bildad: God never twists justice. Your children must have sinned against God and so He punished them as they deserved. Turn and plead with God. If you are honest and pure, God will help you and all your wealth will be nothing compared with what God will give you. God never abandons the faithful – He will let you laugh and shout again.

Job's third friend or 'comforter' was called Zophar. His argument was that Job really deserved to suffer far more.

Zophar: You claim you are pure in the sight of God! How I wish God would answer you! God is punishing you far less than you deserve. God knows which men are worthless, He sees all their evil deeds!

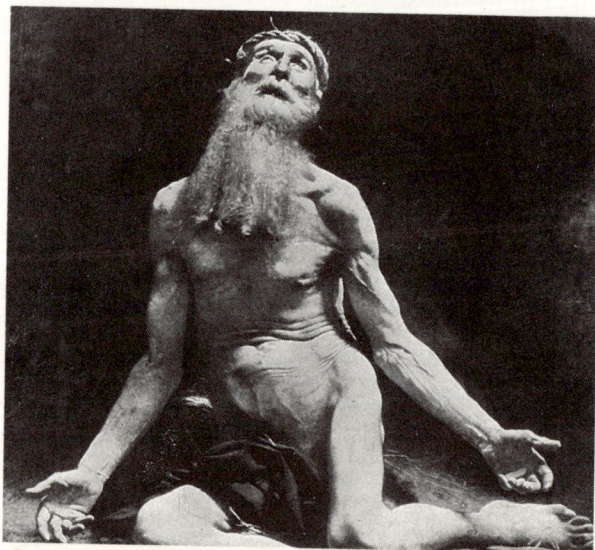

Job

So we discover three answers from the story of Job. Suffering might be:

1 a punishment
2 a way of earning merit or rewards in this life or the next
3 less than we deserve

To talk about...
How do these views compare with the teachings of the world faiths mentioned in the previous unit (Hinduism, Buddhism and Islam)?

Drama
Improvise or write (using your own words) a play which tells the story of Job.

A mystery
In a radio programme, Moshe Davies, a Jewish clergyman, gave this answer when asked for his response to the problem of suffering:

> **"** It is my duty in the world to complete creation. Man is a partner with God in the work of creation. We did not find the world in a state of completeness. This is a world where there are still deficiencies. There is disease. My job is to see what I can do to discover the medicines that will remove it. I don't accept suffering as inevitable. It is part of our process to find the means to combat it and to change the world...
>
> I want to live in a world where there is happiness, where there is joy, where there is pleasure; but I don't want a world where, if I'm walking under a ladder and an object is going to fall on top of my head, something will cancel the natural order of things and the object will be suspended in space until I've passed by. Suffering is part of the process of life, the mystery of life... **"**

CHRISTIANITY

Scapegoats
One Christian answer to the problem of suffering begins by pointing to the 'ceremony of the scapegoat' described in the Old Testament Book of Leviticus.

Much later in the Old Testament, in the Book of Isaiah, there is a poem which describes a mysterious figure called 'the servant of the Lord', who is himself a scapegoat. See Isaiah 53:3–9.

Christians say this prophecy came true in the life and suffering of Jesus. Read through the passage to see how closely it can be said to refer to him.

'I am with you'
Christianity teaches that God does not want or create suffering: suffering is *not* part of His plan. Christians do believe though that good may come out of ill; that new understanding, knowledge, moral strength and the ability to care for others can all result from suffering.

Christians say that suffering is bearable because God Himself (in the person of Jesus) has suffered on the cross and so understands suffering. Christians believe that the example of Jesus gives hope and comfort to those who believe in him.

One Christian clergyman, Canon Trevor Beeson, puts it like this:

> **"** God says, 'Yes, you have got to go through suffering and pain in this life but you don't have to do it on your own. I am in the middle of it with you.' The Christian God is not a remote god. God isn't looking down on us, even pityingly. The cross tells us God is in the midst of our suffering.
>
> There is no easy answer though. It is shrouded in mystery and I think part of growing is being able to accept the mysterious element in life and to know that slick answers are wrong answers. **"**

Write...
Write a poem in honour of someone who has suffered, or try to express your own feelings about the mystery of suffering as a poem.

28·CREMATION

Death is not a subject people like to talk about. We even find ways of avoiding even mentioning the word. We say someone has 'passed on' or 'breathed his last' or even 'kicked the bucket'. Yet the fact that each of us will die is perhaps the one certain thing about the our future. So why do you think death is so difficult to talk about?

Project
Newspapers (both local and national) carry 'obituaries'. These are announcements of deaths and accounts of people's lives. Collect together a selection of newspaper obituaries. Which ones do you think would have pleased the person they are about?

Suppose you die in either forty or sixty years' time. Write your own obituary.

Funerals
When someone dies, there are two particular problems: the disposal of the body and how to comfort the surviving relatives and friends.

Traditionally, there are four ways of disposing of the body: by earth, fire, air and water.

People known as Parsis and also some Tibetans leave the bodies of the dead on the ground to be worn away by exposure. (In parts of Tibet in winter, the ground is too hard to dig and there is little firewood available.)

Burial at sea is practised by some islanders around the world and is also given to those who die at sea. The Book of Common Prayer includes a prayer for this which begins: 'We therefore commit his body to the deep...'

However, the major world faiths normally dispose of the body in the following ways:

	Cremation	Burial
Hinduism	✓	
Buddhism	✓	✓
Judaism		✓
Christianity	✓	✓
Islam		✓
Sikhism	✓	

HINDUISM
In India the climate makes it necessary to hold a funeral very soon after the death has occurred. For Hindus, therefore, cremation usually takes place on the same day as the death.

66 The usual Hindu funeral practice, is that in which the dead body is reduced to ashes by fire. The body is covered with wood, usually sandalwood if it is available. Funeral rites are performed by a priest and the pyre is lit by the eldest son, or by some other male relative if the person had no son. In cities, cremation is sometimes carried out in electric crematoria. Afterwards, the ashes are usually scattered in a river. Relatives often make a pilgrimage to the holy Ganges river to scatter the ashes there.

Soon after death, the body is washed and dressed in special clothes by family members. In a village or small town the body is laid on a stretcher and carried to the cremation ground. It is simply covered with a cloth, often bright red. In a city the body might be carried by family members and friends or a vehicle might be used to take it to the cremation ground.

If a river runs near a city or village, the cremation ground will be situated near the river. Otherwise it is a special area some distance from the village or city that has been set aside for this purpose. Traditionally, the mourners taking the body to the cremation ground should be led by the eldest. Returning home, the youngest person leads the group.

Cremation is a very hygienic way of disposing of the dead, in that fire is an efficient purifier. It is also in keeping with the Hindu belief that it is not the body but the soul that is important. The body may perish but the soul is immortal. **99**

Patricia Bahree

Parts of the Hindu scriptures are said at the time of the cremation, including the lines:

Worn out garments are shed by the body.
Worn out bodies are shed by the dweller.
Within the body, new bodies are donned
by the dweller, like new garments.

To talk about...
What is the great comfort to believers in Hinduism at the time of the death of a loved one?

CREMATION IN BRITAIN
In Britain, cremations take place at a building called a *crematorium*. Inside, a crematorium looks quite like a church, with curtains or doors through which the coffin will disappear.

The body is not taken out of the coffin, and each coffin is burnt individually in a special type of furnace. After about an hour to one and a half hours, the ashes are reduced further to a fine powder-like ash.

Christian cremation
Christians believe in a future life, after death. This is sometimes called 'the resurrection of the body'. Because this was once always taken literally (that is, that one day our bodies would rise up again), Christians used to be very much against cremation. This is not the case nowadays, partly because the disposal of ashes takes less space than does burial in a graveyard.

At Christian cremation, a service may be held either at the crematorium or in a church before the body is taken to the crematorium.

Project
Would you prefer to be buried or cremated? Why?

Conduct an opinion poll in your class or year to see which is the more popular.

To talk about...
1 What do you think of the opinion that these days cremation should be compulsory?
2 If a Christian believes in the literal 'resurrection of the body', would this really mean he or she had to be against cremation?
3 Should a funeral be a sad time for the bereaved?
4 How do different religious beliefs about what happens after death alter the way people feel about it?

29·BURIAL

CHRISTIAN FUNERALS

Christians see death as not the *end* of life but a gateway to a new life. This is a Church of England view of what a funeral is:

❝ A funeral marks the close of a human life on earth. It is the opportunity for friends and family to express their grief, to give thanks for the life which has now completed its journey in this world, and to commend the person who has died into God's keeping. As far back into history as we can penetrate, human beings seem to have felt the need for a ceremonial leave-taking of those who have died.

The funeral service of the Church of England can be very short and quiet with only a few members of the family present, or it can be an occasion of great solemnity with music and hymns and a packed church.

Whether it is held in a parish church or a crematorium chapel, it can be the plain funeral service from the *Prayer Book* or the *Alternative Service Book*, or it can have the addition of hymns, favourite prayers and readings, and an address. In church it can be very appropriately set into the context of a Communion Service. But, whatever the pattern of service, the words and actions all speak of a loving God and the preciousness to Him of every individual human being.

The funeral service will reflect the personality of the one who has died and the circumstances of their death. Feelings of grief, gratitude, joy and sadness often intermingle. Sometimes a sense of tragedy is uppermost, especially when it is a young person who has died; but when it is the end of a long and fruitful life the feelings of thanksgiving can be strongest. ❞

Burial (or 'commital')

❝ The *committal* is the most solemn moment of the funeral service. It takes place either at the graveside or, in the case of a cremation in the crematorium chapel or at the door of the church before the hearse leaves for the crematorium. ❞

This is what happens next, when the service is taken from the Book of Common Prayer.

When they come to the Grave, while the Corpse is made ready to be laid into the earth, the Priest shall say, or the Priest and Clerks shall sing:
MAN that is born of a woman hath but a short time to live, and is full of misery. He cometh up, and is cut down, like a flower; he fleeth as it were a shadow, and never continueth in one stay.

In the midst of life we are in death: of whom may we seek for succour, but of thee, O Lord, who for our sins art justly displeased?

Yet, O Lord God most holy, O Lord most mighty, O holy and most merciful Saviour, deliver us not into the bitter pains of eternal death.

Thou knowest, Lord, the secrets of our hearts; shut not thy merciful ears to our prayer; but spare us, Lord most holy, O God most mighty, O holy and merciful Saviour, thou most worthy Judge eternal, suffer us not, at our last hour, for any pains of death, to fall from thee.

Then, while the earth shall be cast upon the Body by some standing by, the Priest shall say,
FORASMUCH as it hath pleased Almighty God of his great mercy to take unto himself the soul of our dear *brother* here departed, we therefore commit *his* body to the ground; earth to earth, ashes to ashes, dust to dust; in sure and certain hope of the Resurrection to eternal life, through our Lord Jesus Christ; who shall change our vile body, that it may be like unto his glorious body, according to the mighty working, whereby he is able to subdue all things to himself.

❝ The committal can be a very emotional moment. But many who are suffering grief find that, even in their sadness, the words of prayer can lift them towards the experience of Christian rejoicing in the knowledge of life beyond death. The offering of prayer and trust that the person is in God's safe hands can begin the process of healing the grief of loss. **"**

MUSLIM BURIAL

If possible, before a Muslim dies, he or she is reminded of the First Pillar of Islam, the *shahadah* (see unit 12), so that the person will die in faith. When death does occur, the eyes of the deceased are closed and the body is washed (a man's by men, a woman's by women) and wrapped in three white sheets. It is usually taken on a stretcher to the mosque or burial place where prayers are said. Burial is usually without a coffin (so that the body is in contact with the earth) and with the head turned to the right and facing Mecca. If possible, the burial takes place on the day of the death. Women do not usually attend the funeral but visit the grave later.

HUMANISTS

Humanists do not believe in any god but believe that humans are the highest beings that exist. Humanists believe that we should aim to live as morally as we can, and to make our lives as valuable an experience as possible – both for ourselves and for others. Humanists do not believe in life after death.

" Humanists accept death as natural and inevitable and are not afraid of talking about death, dying and funerals. They don't wait until the event happens and accept the traditional religious ritual. They like to sort out the kind of funeral service they would prefer.

Often, a humanist friend will compose a short 'life-story' to be read at the crematorium; many people choose their favourite poems or pieces of music.

Many humanists donate their bodies for medical or teaching purposes; their eyes so that blind people may be offered a corneal graft; their kidneys...because they do not believe that bodies are sacred, but are ours to use and dispose of as we will. **"**

from *The Humanist Dipper*

To talk about...

1 How can a funeral service help the bereaved? What is its purpose?
2 What do you think of the traditional Prayer Book graveside prayers? Are they comforting? Gloomy?
3 Are graveyards and memorials important? Why or why not? Do they deserve special respect?
4 What is 'mourning'? Do you think it right to mourn for the dead? If so, for how long?
5 What music would you like played at your funeral?
6 Do you carry a Donor Card? After your death, would you like your kidneys, eyes, liver and heart to be used in the treatment of others?
7 Why do Humanists often have funeral services? What is the difference in meaning between a religious and a humanist funeral service?
8 Do you believe in life after death?

Write...

Write a short story called 'The Funeral'.

30·HEREAFTER

To talk about...

Would you like to know when you are going to die?

Do you believe you have a 'soul'? If so, what is it? Your brain? Character? Your *self*? Part of God in you?

What is the difference between reincarnation and eternal life?

Do you believe in reincarnation?

Do you believe in eternal life?

If so, in the 'hereafter', will we remember this life? Will we be able to recognise relatives and friends? And communicate with them? Will we know what those still 'alive' are doing?

Do you believe life is an end in itself (as Humanists believe) or do you believe it is a preparation for something else?

LIFE AFTER DEATH

Non-believers sometimes say that the idea of life after death is simply 'pie-in-the-sky'; a wishful dream that death is not the end of everything. Other non-believers have suggested that the idea of an afterlife is a human invention: something that priests and those in authority use to get us to behave in this life.

Those with a religious faith generally do not believe that death is the end of life. Some point to the complex nature of creation and its interlocking patterns. Surely, they say, such a system must indicate life beyond the grave. And, of course, the great teachers of the world's religions (whom their followers believe to be inspired by God) have taught that there is a life beyond death. Christians believe that such an idea is demonstrated by Jesus rising from the dead.

(Remember: the point about a religion is that it is not built on scientific proof but on faith. It means taking the step of saying, 'I believe, even though I can't absolutely prove it to you.')

'Eastern' religions

What are sometimes called the three Eastern religions (Hinduism, Buddhism and Sikhism) have similar beliefs about life after death. All three believe that in some way a being returns to life on earth after death, and eventually 'escapes' this process to become part of God. The aim, therefore, is this escape and the final loss of individual identity.

Hinduism   The Hindu belief in *Karma* and reincarnation is described in Book 2, unit 29.

Buddhism   Buddhists do not believe that an individual soul is re-born in another person, but they do believe that good or evil created in one lifetime is passed on to the next.

Finally, as we overcome greed and selfishness and so avoid all ill or *dukkha* (see unit 11), then the Buddhist believes we shall be released and reach Nirvana, a state of nothingness and freedom.

Sikhism   Sikhs (like Hindus) believe in reincarnation – but what is the final goal for Sikhs?

> 66 It will be peace, and the end, and reaching God. Reaching God means that you are out of the cycle of rebirth and you are attached to God. 99

'Western' religions

The three 'western' religions (Judaism, Christianity, Islam) all teach that each of us has an eternal soul: part of us never dies. Followers of these religions do not generally believe in reincarnation. They believe that each soul survives death and keeps its own separate identity. They also believe in a 'Day of Judgement'. They vary in believing whether this happens for each person soon after their death or whether souls 'sleep' until one final day when all will be judged.

Judaism   Jewish teachers and prophets have not spoken much about life after death, but they do believe that the soul is immortal and that it lives for ever in a way known only to God.

Christianity   (See Book 2, unit 15.) Christians believe in life after death, and in Heaven and Hell:

> What *Heaven* is like, none of us dare say too precisely, but we know that we shall be delighting in the presence and love of God and of the whole company of Heaven, and that whatever is wonderful about life here on earth is only a glimpse of the glory of the life that is to come.
>
> Most Christians would describe *Hell* as separation from that love of God. The separation is never what God wants, it is our own responsibility.

Jesus did speak about Hell as a place of torment, and Christians do believe it is possible to reject God so positively that one sends oneself to Hell. However, they also believe that God is loving and gives us every chance to be with him:

> I believe that I shall be with God in some way. It sounds so amazingly arrogant. It's certainly not because I'm a good person or I deserve it. Or that I'm any better than millions of other people. But it's something that I accept by faith.

Islam   Muslims believe that death is only a step on the way to judgement by God who is both merciful and just. This is how one Muslim explains what will happen:

> Well, when I die the first stage is when I will be buried. The angels will come and ask me the two questions about my religion, whether I believed in Allah, and whether I accept Muhammad as my prophet. If I give those answers correctly, that is to say, 'Yes, I believe in Allah, and that Muhammad is my prophet', the straightforward answers, then I will be required to wait until the Day of Judgement. But until the Day of Judgement there is a long time, so therefore, I will be told at that stage of my likely result on the Day of Judgement, whether I will be going to heaven or hell. So the result is that my punishment may begin, not directly, but indirectly, because of my knowledge of what I'm going to get.

WHAT IT MEANS TO BE...

'Personally, to be a...means to me a host of very important things – things which give meaning to my life and the life of all things around me. My religion explains to me...

'...teaches me how to live my daily life. It teaches me to...'

Suppose a member of each faith were to write two paragraphs beginning as do the two above.

Working in teams of six, write those paragraphs for each believer. Later, teams can split up and re-group 'by religion' to compare their work.

I believe...

If you have worked on Book 1 of this *Course*, you may have written out your own creed; your statement of what you believe (unit 2). Do you still believe the same things?

Once again, try writing your own statement of belief: 'I believe...'

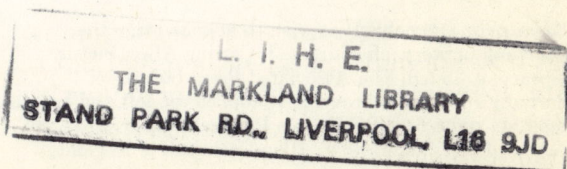

LINKED

...SIONS

As we reach the end of this *Course*, we can perhaps summarise what we have found out. Working either alone or in pairs, make your own large copy of this table. Then fill it in.

Religion	God or gods	Founder or messenger	Holy Book	Place of Worship	Main Festivals	Pilgrimage	Rules for living

First published 1987

Published by
MACMILLAN EDUCATION LTD
Houndmills, Basingstoke, Hampshire RG 21 2XS
and London
Companies and representatives
throughout the world

Designed by Nina J.Nadolski-Birks

Printed in Hong Kong

British Library Cataloguing in Publication Data
Self, David
Living a faith.——(Macmillan religious education courses; bk. 3)
1. Religions
I. Title
291   BL80.2
ISBN 0–333–39218–3

Acknowledgements

The author and publishers wish to acknowledge the following photograph sources: J. Catling Allen Picture Library, p. 38 left; The Associated Press Ltd, p. 55; Barnaby's Picture Library, p. 18 top, 35 top left and bottom right, 45 right, 61; BBC Hulton Picture Library, p. 43, 56; Camera Press Ltd, p. 10; J. Allen Cash Ltd, p. 28 right; Catholic Pictorial, p. 21; Stephanie Colasanti, p. 48; Commission for Racial Equality, p. 28 centre; Michael Edwards, p. 23; Federation of British Crematorium Authorities, p. 59 right; Sally and Richard Greenhill, p. 51; Sonia Halliday Photographs, p. 35 top right; John and Penny Hubley, p. 4, 53; Hutchison Photographic Library, p. 38 right, 47 left; Rodney Jennings, p. 6, 29, 45 left; Jewish Education Bureau, p. 31; Keep Sunday Special Campaign, p. 30; Methodist Church Press Service, p. 20; Ann and Bury Peerless, p. 17, 18 bottom, 47 right; The Photo Source, p. 54; Picturepoint Ltd, p. 27; Punch, p. 14; David Richardson, p. 7, 8, 9, 12, 13, 16; Religious Society of Friends, p. 36 bottom left; Royal National Institute for the Deaf, p. 28 centre; Salvation Army, p. 36 top; The Slide Centre, p. 35 bottom left; Royal National Institute for the Deaf, p. 28 left; Salvation Army, p. 36 top; The Slide Centre, p. 35 bottom left; Topham Picture Library, p. 37; United Society for the Propagation of the Gospel, p. 36 bottom right; Zefa Picture

The author and publishers wish to thank the following who have kindly given permission for the use of copyright material: Behrman House Inc. for extracts from *When a Jew Celebrates* by Harry Gersh; Central Board of Finance of the Church of England for extracts from the Baptism and Confirmation services in *The Alternative Service Book 1980* and from 'Christening Your Baby', Getting Married in Church' and 'Funerals' in *Explaining the Church of England*, publications of General Synod; Christian Aid for 'Banishing Poverty' from *Worship Suggestions for Christian Aid Week 1983*; Marianne Cook for an excerpt from a play 'Going Away from the Family' broadcast in *Religious Education*, BBC School Radio, 7.3.80; Eyre and Spottiswoode (Publishers) Ltd for Crown copyright material from *The Book of Common Prayer of 1662*; Grevatt & Grevatt, Dermot Killingley and Hari Shukla for extracts from *A Handbook of Hinduism for Teachers* edited by Dermot Killingley; Michael Quicke for quoted material on baptism in the Baptist Church.

The publishers have made every effort to trace the copyright holders, but where they have failed to do so they will be pleased to make the necessary arrangements at the first opportunity.